Bet Is for B'reishit

Hebrew for Adults
Book 3

Linda Motzkin
The author of
Aleph Isn't Tough and
Aleph Isn't Enough

Hara Person, series editor

The author gratefully acknowledges the following for permission to reprint previously published material:

ACUM LTD: "Written in pencil in the sealed freight car" by Dan Pagis. Copyright © by Dan Pagis and Acum. Reprinted by permission of Acum Ltd.

HARPERCOLLINS PUBLISHERS: Excerpts from *Commentary on the Torah* by Richard Elliott Friedman. © 2001 by HarperCollins Publishers. Reprinted by permission of HarperCollins Publishers Inc.

JEWISH PUBLICATION SOCIETY: Excerpts from *JPS Hebrew-English Tanakh: The Traditional Hebrew Text and the New JPS Translation*, Second Edition © 1999 by the Jewish Publication Society. Reprinted by permission of Jewish Publication Society.

KOREN PUBLISHERS JERUSALEM, LTD.: Excerpts from *The Jerusalem Bible* copyright © 1998 by Koren Publishers Jerusalem. Reprinted by permission of Koren Publishers Jerusalem, Ltd.

MESORAH PUBLICATIONS, LTD.: Reproduced from *The Chumash*, The Stone Edition, Artscroll Series, edited by Rabbi Nosson Scherman. Copyright © 1993, 1994 by Mesorah Publications, Ltd. With permission from the copyright holders Artscroll/Mesorah Publications, Ltd.

SCHOCKEN BOOKS: From *The Five Books of Moses* by Everett Fox, copyright © 1983, 1986, 1990, 1995 by Schocken Books. Used by permission of Schocken Books, a division of Random House, Inc.

SOUNDS WRITE PRODUCTIONS, INC.: "L'chi Lach" text by Debbie Friedman and Savina Teubal from "And You Shall Be a Blessing." Copyright © 1988 by Deborah Lynn Friedman (ASCAP), (San Diego, Calif.: Sounds Write Productions, Inc., 1988). Reprinted by permission of Sounds Write Productions, Inc. (ASCAP)

A Note on the Translations

The translations provided in this book in the Additional Reading and Translation Practice sections are as close to literal as possible, so that you can easily compare them with the original language. In some instances, a word or phrase is followed by another possible translation that is included in brackets {like this}. A different style of brackets [like this] occasionally appears in this book and is used to indicate words not included in the Hebrew that have been inserted for clarity in the English translation.

Moreover, the terms יְיָ and יְהוָֹה can be translated in several different ways, as seen in the Torah text translations cited in each odd numbered chapter. In our own translations, we have chosen to translate these terms as "Eternal One," "The Eternal One," "The Eternal." Likewise, in our own translations we have chosen to translate the Hebrew pronouns referring to God not as "He" or "Him" (nor "It" or "Its") but as "God" and "God's" followed by brackets {like this} indicating the literal masculine translation.

Table of Contents

Acknowledgments

Bet Is for B'reshit is the third book in the UAHC Hebrew for Adults Series. Along with the first and second books, *Aleph Isn't Tough* and *Aleph Isn't Enough*, it owes its existence to the vision of Rabbi Eric Yoffie, President of the UAHC, who inaugurated a historic campaign in 1996 to revive Hebrew literacy throughout the Reform Movement. The UAHC Hebrew Literacy Task Force, co-chaired by Rabbis Jan Katzew and Lawrence Raphael, was convened to respond to this challenge and provided direction and input in the development of this series.

Many rabbis and educators in the field of Hebrew language instruction agreed to pilot this text in adult classes in their communities and provided valuable perspectives and suggestions regarding adult Hebrew learning. I greatly appreciate the feedback provided by the teachers and students in the following congregations: Temple Beth El, Somerville, NJ; Congregation Sinai, Milwaukee, WI; Temple Beth Israel, Altoona, PA; Temple Society of Concord, Syracuse, NY; The Scarsdale Synagogue-Tremont Temple, Scarsdale, NY; Temple Emanu-el, Westfield, NJ; Isaac M. Wise Temple, Cincinnati, OH; Congregation Solel, Highland Park, IL; Temple B'nai Torah, Bellevue, WA; The Temple, Louisville, KY; and Congregation Etz Chaim, Merced, CA. I am particularly grateful to Sarah Gluck, David Blumberg, Iris Petroff, and Rabbi Arlene Schuster for their willingness to share their ideas and experiences teaching the experimental material.

A portion of this book was written while I was on sabbatical in Costa Rica. I am grateful to my congregation, Temple Sinai of Saratoga Springs, New York, for giving me six months away to work on this project. I am also grateful to Congregacion B'nei Israel in San Jose, Costa Rica, and to the Monteverde Society of Friends in Monteverde, Costa Rica, for the warm and welcoming way they embraced my family during our time with them.

I have been blessed in my community in Saratoga Springs, New York, with a wonderful group of dedicated and enthusiastic students, who have given me the opportunity to pilot this text at Temple Sinai. For their hard work, their good humor, and their willingness to keep coming back for more week after week, my tremendous thanks and affection go to Lollie Abramson Stark, Dan Balmuth, Rita Balmuth, Cathy DeDe, Eleanor deVries, Diana Fenton, Carla Gordon, Daniel Graham, Dianna Goodwin, Sue Joki, Lisa Kingston, Tina Marlowe, Deborah Meyers, Art Ruben, Robin Sacks, and Naomi Tannen.

At the UAHC Press, there were a number of people who assisted in various steps toward the publication of this book. Rabbi Hara Person, Editorial Director of the UAHC Press, guided this third book to the light of day with the same combination of constructive feedback, gentle suggestions, and clarity of vision that she brought to the editing of the first two books. It has been a pleasure to work with her at every stage of this process. Those who assisted in all the various aspects of the production of this book include Rabbi Dan Freelander, Rabbi Jan Katzew, Ken Gesser, Joel Eglash, Liane Broido, Annie Belford, and Debra Hirsch Corman.

And last, but most important of all, my gratitude and appreciation go to my family: to my husband and co-rabbi, Rabbi Jonathan Rubenstein, for the countless ways in which he makes me and my life better than either would be without him; and to our three terrific children, Rachel, Ari, and Shira. Their love and support are my life's greatest blessings.

Welcome

בְּרוּכִים הַבָּאִים

This book provides a continuation of your study of classical Hebrew through an exploration of selected passages from the Torah. *Bet Is for B'reishit* is divided into five units, each consisting of two chapters that are organized around the same Torah Study Text. In the first chapter of each unit, the Torah Study Text is introduced, along with translations, vocabulary, two new Hebrew roots, and Torah commentary. In the second chapter of each unit, Building Blocks (grammatical concepts) derived from the Torah Study Text are presented, along with additional reading and translation practice. (There is one exception to this division that you will see in Chapter 3). מַזָּל טוֹב on having reached the level where you can begin to study Torah in Hebrew!

Torah Study Text: Genesis 1:1–5

The Torah opens with the account of God's creation of the world in seven days: six days of creative work and the seventh day of rest. The following are the first five verses of the Torah, describing the first day of Creation. This passage contains many words, Hebrew roots, and grammatical concepts that have not yet been introduced. You are not expected to be able to translate this entire passage. Read the Hebrew below to see how many of the words you can recognize. Underline or circle the words, roots, endings, and prefixes that you know.

¹בְּרֵאשִׁית בָּרָא אֱלֹהִים אֵת הַשָּׁמַיִם וְאֵת הָאָרֶץ: ²וְהָאָרֶץ הָיְתָה

תֹהוּ וָבֹהוּ וְחֹשֶׁךְ עַל־פְּנֵי תְהוֹם וְרוּחַ אֱלֹהִים מְרַחֶפֶת עַל־פְּנֵי

הַמָּיִם: ³וַיֹּאמֶר אֱלֹהִים יְהִי אוֹר וַיְהִי־אוֹר: ⁴וַיַּרְא אֱלֹהִים אֶת־הָאוֹר

כִּי־טוֹב וַיַּבְדֵּל אֱלֹהִים בֵּין הָאוֹר וּבֵין הַחֹשֶׁךְ: ⁵וַיִּקְרָא אֱלֹהִים

לָאוֹר יוֹם וְלַחֹשֶׁךְ קָרָא לָיְלָה וַיְהִי־עֶרֶב וַיְהִי־בֹקֶר יוֹם אֶחָד:

Translating the Torah Study Text

The Torah Study Text, Genesis 1:1–5, is reprinted below. Underneath each Hebrew word is a literal translation (except for the word אֵת, which has no English translation). This literal translation of the individual words does not produce a smooth English reading of the passage. In order to arrange the words into meaningful English sentences, it is necessary to draw upon your knowledge of the building blocks of the Hebrew language. It is also necessary to make choices between various possible translations of individual words and phrases.

Using your knowledge of the building blocks of the Hebrew language and the meanings of the words provided below, translate this passage into clear English sentences. Write your translation on the lines following the text. This selection includes some grammatical forms and vocabulary that have not yet been introduced. You will need to rely, in part, on the translations provided.

1 בְּרֵאשִׁית בָּרָא אֱלֹהִים אֵת הַשָּׁמַיִם וְאֵת הָאָרֶץ:

| in/with/at beginning (of) | created | God | the sky/heavens | and | the earth/land |

---

2 וְהָאָרֶץ הָיְתָה תֹהוּ וָבֹהוּ וְחֹשֶׁךְ עַל־ פְּנֵי

| and the earth/land | was | nothingness and void | and darkness | over/upon | face/surface |

תְהוֹם וְרוּחַ אֱלֹהִים מְרַחֶפֶת עַל־ פְּנֵי הַמָּיִם:

| deep | and wind/spirit | God | hovering | over/upon | face/surface | the water |

---

3 וַיֹּאמֶר אֱלֹהִים יְהִי אוֹר וַיְהִי־ אוֹר: **4** וַיַּרְא אֱלֹהִים

| and said | God | let [there] be | light | and [there] was | light | and saw | God |

אֶת־הָאוֹר כִּי־ טוֹב וַיַּבְדֵּל אֱלֹהִים בֵּין הָאוֹר וּבֵין

| the light | that | good | and separated | God | between | the light | and between |

---

5 וַיִּקְרָא אֱלֹהִים לָאוֹר יוֹם וְלַחֹשֶׁךְ קָרָא הַחֹשֶׁךְ:

| and called | God | {to} the light | day | and {to} the darkness | called | the darkness |

לָֽיְלָה וַֽיְהִי־ עֶרֶב וַֽיְהִי־ בֹקֶר יוֹם אֶחָֽד׃

night	and [there] was	evening	and [there] was	morning	day	one

Translations

Translation from one language to another is not an exact science but a subjective art. Every translation is an interpretation of the original text, as there are often several possible ways that a given verse, or even a single word, can be understood. The following translations of our Torah Study Text: Genesis 1:1–5 all take slightly different approaches to the text. Compare your translation above with these Torah translations. Notice the subtle differences between each of these translations and your own.

[1]When God began to create heaven and earth—[2]the earth being unformed and void, with darkness over the surface of the deep and a wind from God sweeping over the water—[3]God said, "Let there be light"; and there was light. [4]God saw that the light was good, and God separated the light from the darkness. [5]God called the light Day, and the darkness He called Night. And there was evening and there was morning, a first day.

JPS HEBREW-ENGLISH TANAKH: THE TRADITIONAL HEBREW TEXT AND THE NEW JPS TRANSLATION—2D ED. PHILADELPHIA: THE JEWISH PUBLICATION SOCIETY, 1999.

[1]In the beginning of God's creating the heavens and the earth—[2]when the earth was astonishingly empty, with darkness upon the surface of the deep, and the Divine Presence hovered upon the surface of the waters—[3]God said, "Let there be light," and there was light. [4]God saw that the light was good, and God separated between the light and the darkness. [5]God called to the light: "Day," and to the darkness He called: "Night." And there was evening and there was morning, one day.

THE CHUMASH, ARTSCROLL SERIES, STONE EDITION. BROOKLYN: MESORAH PUBLICATIONS, 1993.

[1]At the beginning of God's creating of the heavens and the earth,
[2]when the earth was wild and waste,
darkness over the face of Ocean,
rushing-spirit of God hovering over the face of the waters—

[3]God said: Let there be light! And there was light.
[4]God saw the light: that it was good.
God separated the light from the darkness.

⁵*God called the light: Day! and the darkness he called: Night!*
There was setting, there was dawning: one day.

THE FIVE BOOKS OF MOSES: A NEW TRANSLATION WITH INTRODUCTIONS,
COMMENTARY, AND NOTES BY EVERETT FOX. NEW YORK: SCHOCKEN BOOKS, 1995.

*In the beginning God created the heaven and the earth. And the earth was without
form and void; and darkness was on the face of the deep. And a wind from God moved
over the surface of the waters. And God said, Let there be light: and there was light.
And God saw the light, that it was good: and God divided the light from the darkness.
And God called the light Day, and the darkness he called Night. And there was
evening and there was morning, one day.*

THE JERUSALEM BIBLE, PUBLISHED FOR THE NAHUM ZEEV WILLIAMS FAMILY
FOUNDATION AT HECHAL SHLOMO, JERUSALEM. JERUSALEM: KOREN PUBLISHERS
JERUSALEM LTD., 1969.

Vocabulary

Locate each of the following words in the Torah Study Text: Genesis 1:1–5.

darkness *m*	—	חֹשֶׁךְ
face, faces, surface *m and f, pl*	—	פָּנִים
spirit, wind *m and f*	—	רוּחַ
water, waters *m, pl*	—	מַיִם
light *m*	—	אוֹר
between, among	—	בֵּין
evening *m*	—	עֶרֶב
morning *m*	—	בֹּקֶר

Notes on the Vocabulary

1. חֹשֶׁךְ, "darkness," is the ninth of the Ten Plagues of the Exodus story, enumerated at the Passover seder.
2. The words פָּנִים, "face/faces/surface," and מַיִם, "water," are grammatically plural words that can have a singular or plural meaning in English. The word-pair form of פָּנִים is פְּנֵי, "face of."
3. As with other Hebrew prepositions, the word בֵּין has endings attached when it is followed by a pronoun such as "you" or "us" or "him":

between/among us	—	בֵּינֵינוּ
between/among you *m sg*	—	בֵּינְךָ

4. The words עֶרֶב and בֹּקֶר appear in the greetings עֶרֶב טוֹב, "good evening," and בֹּקֶר טוֹב "good morning."

The basic meaning of the root א־מ־ר is "say," "utter," or "tell." This root follows the ▢◌ֹו▢ participle pattern. The following are the four participle forms:

אוֹמֵר *m sg* אוֹמֶרֶת *f sg* אוֹמְרִים *m pl* אוֹמְרוֹת *f pl*

The root א־מ־ר appears only once in the Torah Study Text:

(verse 3)

And God said	—	וַיֹּאמֶר אֱלֹהִים

The following words, both ancient and modern, are derived from the root א־מ־ר:

utterance, speech, word	—	אֹמֶר
word, utterance, saying	—	אִמְרָה
article, essay; *also* injunction, decree	—	מַאֲמָר
statement	—	אֲמָרָה
saying, talk	—	אֲמִירָה

The basic meaning of the root ה־י־ה is "be" or "exist." As explained in Chapter 1 of *Aleph Isn't Enough*, there is no present-tense form of the verb "to be" in Hebrew. There is no participle form of the root ה־י־ה.

The root ה־י־ה appears in following verses in the Torah Study Text. In some words formed from this root, the final letter ה drops out. In the word הָיְתָה in verse 2, the final letter ה of ה־י־ה has switched to the letter ת, with another ה ending attached.

(verse 2)

and the earth was void and nothingness	—	וְהָאָרֶץ הָיְתָה תֹהוּ וָבֹהוּ

(verse 3)

let [there] be light	—	יְהִי אוֹר

(verse 3)

and [there] was light	—	וַיְהִי אוֹר

and [there] was evening and [there] was morning   —   וַיְהִי עֶרֶב וַיְהִי בֹקֶר

Torah Commentary

Much of Torah commentary arises from the fact that Hebrew words and phrases can be understood in more than one way. Often a commentary stems from a detail in the Hebrew text that may be lost or obscured in an English translation. Above each of the following selections, the Hebrew detail giving rise to the commentary is explained.

The Torah begins not with בָּרֵאשִׁית, "in **the** beginning," but with בְּרֵאשִׁית, "in beginning" or "in a beginning." This would suggest that there was not only one beginning.

In other words, even after the world was created, we are still at the beginning, at the point of creation. If an artisan makes an object, that object now has an independent existence. The world, though, requires a renewal of its strength each instant by God to keep it in existence.

R. BUNIM OF PSHISCHA, AS QUOTED IN *TORAH GEMS*, COMP. AHARON YAAKOV GREENBERG, TRANS. RABBI DR. SHMUEL HIMELSTEIN. TEL AVIV AND BROOKLYN: YAVNEH PUBLISHING HOUSE, CHEMED BOOKS, 1998.

The Torah begins with the letter ב, the second letter of the Hebrew alphabet.

There is ... [a] reason for creating the world using the letter ב. This explanation communicates the underlying motif for the world's creation and its continued existence. The numerical equivalent of the letter ב is two. This alludes to harmony and unity. When people live together, when two individuals work together—not as separate units—the world has meaning and life has value. People must always think of others, not only of themselves.

HORAV DOVID SHNEUR, CITED IN *PENINIM ON THE TORAH*, 6TH SERIES, BY RABBI A. LEIB SCHEINBAUM. CLEVELAND HEIGHTS: PENINIM PUBLICATIONS, 2000.

In verse 5, the text states וַיְהִי עֶרֶב, "and there was evening," without ever stating יְהִי עֶרֶב, "let there be evening."

Rabbi Yehudah ben Rabbi Shimon said: "'Let there be evening' is not written here, but 'and there was evening'; hence we know that a time-order existed before this." Rabbi Abbahu said: "This proves that the blessed Holy One went on creating worlds and destroying them—until creating this one and declaring, 'This one pleases Me; those did not please Me.'"

B'REISHIT RABBAH 3:7

Exercises

1. Make flash cards for each of the new vocabulary words and Hebrew roots introduced in this chapter, or use the flash card set published as a companion to this book. Review the cards to learn all of them.

2. Draw a line connecting each Hebrew word to its English translation. For some words, there can be more than one correct translation.

<table>
<tr><td>water</td><td>חֹשֶׁךְ</td></tr>
<tr><td>light</td><td>בֵּין</td></tr>
<tr><td>between</td><td>אוֹר</td></tr>
<tr><td>spirit</td><td>רוּחַ</td></tr>
<tr><td>face</td><td>מַיִם</td></tr>
<tr><td>morning</td><td>פָּנִים</td></tr>
<tr><td>wind</td><td>עֶרֶב</td></tr>
<tr><td>darkness</td><td>בֹּקֶר</td></tr>
<tr><td>evening</td><td></td></tr>
<tr><td>faces</td><td></td></tr>
</table>

3. The following are singular and plural forms of nouns introduced as vocabulary in this chapter. Draw a line connecting each plural noun to its singular form. Translate both into English.

_____	אוֹרוֹת	רוּחַ	_____
_____	בְּקָרִים	אוֹר	_____
_____	רוּחוֹת		
_____	עֲרָבִים	עֶרֶב	_____
_____	אוֹרִים	בֹּקֶר	_____

The following exercises use words and roots introduced in this chapter and in *Aleph Isn't Enough*. All words and roots from *Aleph Isn't Enough* are included in the Glossary at the back of this book.

4. Read and translate the following groups of words.

b. רוּחַ גְּדוֹלָה _____	a. בֹּקֶר טוֹב _____
רוּחַ אֵל _____	עֶרֶב טוֹב _____
רוּחַ חַיִּים _____	לַיְלָה טוֹב _____
רוּחַ קָדְשׁוֹ _____	שֵׁם טוֹב _____
רוּחוֹת הַשָּׁמַיִם _____	יוֹם טוֹב _____

d. אוֹר פָּנֶיךָ _____	c. בֵּינְךָ _____
בְּאוֹר פָּנֶיךָ _____	בֵּינֵיכֶם _____
פְּנֵי הָאָדוֹן _____	בֵּינֵינוּ _____
פְּנֵי אֱלֹהִים _____	בֵּינוֹ _____
פְּנֵי הָאֲדָמָה _____	בֵּין בְּנֵי יִשְׂרָאֵל _____

f. לֶחֶם וָמַיִם _____	e. אוֹר הַבֹּקֶר _____
מַיִם חַיִּים _____	אוֹר לַגּוֹיִים _____
מַיִם רַבִּים _____	חֹשֶׁךְ וָאוֹר _____
מַיִם קְדוֹשִׁים _____	אֶרֶץ חֹשֶׁךְ _____
מֵי מִצְרַיִם _____	יוֹם חֹשֶׁךְ _____

5. Identify the root of each of the following participles, and whether the participle form is masculine or feminine, singular or plural. Translate the meaning of the root. Notice that some of these participles begin with the prefix "מ", introduced in Chapter 10 of *Aleph Isn't Enough*.

m/f	sing/pl	Translation	Root	Participle
_____	_____	_____	_____	אוֹמֵר
_____	_____	_____	_____	מְבָרֵךְ
_____	_____	_____	_____	מְהַלֵּל
_____	_____	_____	_____	עוֹזֵר
_____	_____	_____	_____	אוֹמְרִים
_____	_____	_____	_____	מְדַבְּרִים
_____	_____	_____	_____	מוֹלְכִים
_____	_____	_____	_____	בּוֹרֵא
_____	_____	_____	_____	שׁוֹמְרִים
_____	_____	_____	_____	בּוֹחֵר

EXTRA CREDIT

A Day in Jewish Time

The earth spins on its axis one full revolution every twenty-four hours. We experience this movement on earth as the twenty-four-hour cycle of day and night. This movement is continuous; there is no moment when it begins or ends. The secular definition of a new day beginning after midnight is an arbitrary definition; a new day could just as easily have been said to begin at 1:00 A.M.

There are, however, two times during each twenty-four-hour period when an observable change occurs in the natural environment: sunrise and sunset. Either of these would be a logical time to designate as the transition from one day to the next. Jewish tradition adopted sunset, not sunrise, as the time for reckoning the start of each new day. This is one understanding of the phrase included in verse 5 of this chapter's Torah Study Text, and repeated at the end of each of the six days of Creation: וַיְהִי־עֶרֶב וַיְהִי־בֹקֶר, "There was evening and there was morning, [one day, a second day, a third day...]." Because עֶרֶב, "evening," precedes בֹקֶר, "morning," in each of these verses, the evening precedes the morning in the Jewish way of delineating each day. Hence, it is evening (sunset) that marks the beginning of Shabbat and every Jewish holiday, because that is when each new Jewish day begins.

Torah Study Text: Vocabulary and Root Review

This unit's Torah Study Text, Genesis 1:1–5, is reprinted below, highlighting the new vocabulary words as well as the words formed from the new Hebrew roots introduced in Chapter 1. Read this passage again, recalling the meaning of each of the highlighted words or roots.

בְּרֵאשִׁית בָּרָא אֱלֹהִים אֵת הַשָּׁמַיִם וְאֵת הָאָרֶץ: ²וְהָאָרֶץ הָיְתָה תֹהוּ וָבֹהוּ וְחֹשֶׁךְ עַל־פְּנֵי תְהוֹם וְרוּחַ אֱלֹהִים מְרַחֶפֶת עַל־פְּנֵי הַמָּיִם: ³וַיֹּאמֶר אֱלֹהִים יְהִי אוֹר וַיְהִי־אוֹר: ⁴וַיַּרְא אֱלֹהִים אֶת־הָאוֹר כִּי־טוֹב וַיַּבְדֵּל אֱלֹהִים בֵּין הָאוֹר וּבֵין הַחֹשֶׁךְ: ⁵וַיִּקְרָא אֱלֹהִים לָאוֹר יוֹם וְלַחֹשֶׁךְ קָרָא לָיְלָה וַיְהִי־עֶרֶב וַיְהִי־בֹקֶר יוֹם אֶחָד:

Building Blocks

Tenses in Hebrew

In classical Hebrew, there is no past or future tense. Instead, there are "perfect" verbs, which describe action that has been completed, and "imperfect" verbs, which describe ongoing, incompleted action.

Perfect Verbs

There are many different verb patterns in Hebrew. The simplest perfect verb pattern uses the three letters of the root without any prefixes or suffixes to produce the הוא form of the verb:

A common variation in the vowels is ⬛ ⬛ ⬛. Since a perfect verb describes action that has been completed, it can be translated into English in several different ways, as in the following example:

הוּא בָּרָא.

He created. He did create. He was creating. He had created. He has created.

Imperfect Verbs

The simplest imperfect verb pattern uses the three letters of the root with the prefix יְ to produce the הוּא form of the verb. Various vowel combinations may appear under the root letters:

An imperfect verb can be translated into English to indicate the future tense, ongoing incompleted action, or action that is wished or urged:

הוּא יַעֲשֶׂה

He will make.   He may make.   May he make.   Let him make.

The Reversing *Vav*

In *Aleph Isn't Enough*, we introduced the prefix וְ meaning "and." The prefix וְ is also the primary marker of a form characteristic of biblical Hebrew, in which what looks much like an imperfect verb should be understood as a perfect verb or vice versa. When this occurs, the translation may or may not include the word "and." (Remember that there are several other ways that each verb can be translated in addition to the translations given below.)

perfect: [he] said	—	אָמַר
imperfect: [he] will say	—	יֹאמַר
imperfect with reversing vav: [he] said *or* [and he] said	—	וַיֹּאמֶר

Notice the dot in the י in the word וַיֹּאמֶר. A dot often appears in the י prefix of an imperfect verb when a reversing vav is attached.

When a reversing *vav* is attached to an imperfect verb with the final root letter ה, the final ה drops out:

imperfect: [it, he] will be *or* let [him, it] be	—	יִהְיֶה
imperfect: [it, he] was	—	וַיְהִי

Sometimes the final letter ה drops out even when there is no reversing *vav* so as to clearly express the speaker's wish or judgment about a situation:

let [it] be	—	יְהִי
let light be *or* let [there] be light	—	יְהִי אוֹר

Translating Tenses

The biblical Hebrew participle, perfect, and imperfect verb forms do not correspond exactly to our English present, past, and future tenses. Moreover, the absence of a Hebrew verb in a biblical verse does not necessarily signify the present tense. When translating biblical Hebrew into English, the tense must be determined by the context. The following examples come from this unit's Torah Study Text.

(verse 2)

and darkness [was] over/upon the face/surface of the deep	—	וְחֹשֶׁךְ עַל־פְּנֵי תְהוֹם
hovering (f sg participle from the root ר־ח־ף)	—	מְרַחֶפֶת
and wind/spirit of God [was] hovering	—	וְרוּחַ אֱלֹהִים מְרַחֶפֶת

(verse 4)

and God saw the light that [it was] good	—	וַיַּרְא אֱלֹהִים אֶת־הָאוֹר כִּי־טוֹב

Torah Study Text with Building Blocks

Following is this unit's Torah Study Text, Genesis 1:1–5, reprinted with the new Building Blocks highlighted. Reread this text, noting the appearance of perfect and imperfect verbs, with and without the reversing *vav*. A translation is provided below for only the highlighted Building Blocks. Remember that there could be other possible translations. For a translation of the entire passage, refer back to Chapter 1.

בְּרֵאשִׁית **בָּרָא** אֱלֹהִים אֵת הַשָּׁמַיִם וְאֵת הָאָרֶץ: ²וְהָאָרֶץ הָיְתָה
תֹהוּ וָבֹהוּ וְחֹשֶׁךְ עַל־פְּנֵי תְהוֹם וְרוּחַ אֱלֹהִים מְרַחֶפֶת עַל־פְּנֵי
הַמָּיִם: ³**וַיֹּאמֶר** אֱלֹהִים **יְהִי** אוֹר **וַיְהִי־**אוֹר: ⁴**וַיַּרְא** אֱלֹהִים אֶת־
הָאוֹר כִּי־טוֹב **וַיַּבְדֵּל** אֱלֹהִים בֵּין הָאוֹר וּבֵין הַחֹשֶׁךְ: ⁵**וַיִּקְרָא**
אֱלֹהִים לָאוֹר יוֹם וְלַחֹשֶׁךְ **קָרָא** לָיְלָה **וַיְהִי־**עֶרֶב **וַיְהִי־**בֹקֶר
יוֹם אֶחָד:

[he] created	—	בָּרָא
[and he] said	—	וַיֹּאמֶר
let [it] be	—	יְהִי
[and it] was	—	וַיְהִי

[and he] saw	—	וַיַּרְא
[and he] separated	—	וַיַּבְדֵּל
[and he] called	—	וַיִּקְרָא
[he] called	—	קָרָא

הוּא Forms

The following chart includes the participle, perfect, and imperfect הוּא forms for every root introduced thus far that follows the simple pattern. This chart presents the regular vowels for each form, but alternate or irregular vowels sometimes appear in biblical texts. Keep in mind that this chart is included for enrichment only. It is not necessary to memorize these forms.

It may be helpful to notice the following variations: in many roots that begin with the letter י or the letter נ, such as י־צ־א and נ־ת־ן, that first root letter י or נ drops out in the imperfect form: תֵּצֵא, תִּתֵּן.

	Imperfect	Perfect	Participle	Root	
	יֶאֱהַב	אָהַב	אוֹהֵב	א־ה־ב	love
	יֹאכַל	אָכַל	אוֹכֵל	א־כ־ל	eat
	יֹאמַר	אָמַר	אוֹמֵר	א־מ־ר	say
	יִבְחַר	בָּחַר	בּוֹחֵר	ב־ח־ר	choose
	יִבְרָא	בָּרָא	בּוֹרֵא	ב־ר־א	create
	יִהְיֶה	הָיָה	–	ה־י־ה	be
	יִזְכֹּר	זָכַר	זוֹכֵר	ז־כ־ר	remember
(irregular imperfect— root letter י missing) {	יֵצֵא	יָצָא	יוֹצֵא	י־צ־א	go out
	יִמְלֹךְ	מָלַךְ	מוֹלֵךְ	מ־ל־ךְ	rule
(irregular imperfect— root letter נ missing) {	יִתֵּן	נָתַן	נוֹתֵן	נ־ת־ן	give
	יַעֲזֹר	עָזַר	עוֹזֵר	ע־ז־ר	help
	יַעֲשֶׂה	עָשָׂה	עוֹשֶׂה	ע־שׂ־ה	make, do
	יִרְפָּא	רָפָא	רוֹפֵא	ר־פ־א	heal
	יִשְׁמַע	שָׁמַע	שׁוֹמֵעַ	שׁ־מ־ע	hear
	יִשְׁמֹר	שָׁמַר	שׁוֹמֵר	שׁ־מ־ר	guard, keep

CHAPTER 2

Additional Reading and Translation Practice

Translate the following excerpts from the Bible and the prayer book, using the extra vocabulary words provided. Other words were introduced in this chapter or in *Aleph Isn't Enough* and are included in the Glossary at the end of this book. Check your translations against the English translations that follow.

1. עֹשֶׂה שָׁלוֹם—The last line of the *Kaddish* prayer has become a song in its own right and is included in the Reform liturgy in weekday, Shabbat, and holiday services, where it is generally sung after a period of silent prayer. The root ע־שׂ־ה appears as both a participle (used as a noun in a word pair) and as an imperfect verb.

heights	—	מְרוֹמִים
[all of you] say *(a plural command form)*	—	אִמְרוּ

עֹשֶׂה שָׁלוֹם בִּמְרוֹמָיו, הוּא יַעֲשֶׂה שָׁלוֹם, עָלֵינוּ וְעַל כָּל יִשְׂרָאֵל,
וְאִמְרוּ אָמֵן:

_____

_____

2. From אֲדוֹן עוֹלָם—This well-known hymn in praise of God is sung at the conclusion of Shabbat and holiday services. It consists of ten lines, often melodically divided into five verses.

Following is the second verse. The root מ־ל־ך appears as an imperfect verb; the root ה־י־ה appears as both a perfect and imperfect verb.

after	—	אַחֲרֵי
ending	—	כִּכְלוֹת
alone, by himself	—	לְבַדּוֹ
awesome	—	נוֹרָא
is present, exists, is	—	הֹוֶה
splendor, glory	—	תִּפְאָרָה

וְאַחֲרֵי כִּכְלוֹת הַכֹּל, לְבַדּוֹ יִמְלֹךְ נוֹרָא.
וְהוּא הָיָה, וְהוּא הֹוֶה, וְהוּא יִהְיֶה, בְּתִפְאָרָה.

3. From the Torah Service (biblical phrases)—This passage from the beginning of the Torah Service is a composite of biblical phrases from Psalm 10:16—יְיָ מֶלֶךְ; Psalm 93:1—יְיָ מָלָךְ; and Exodus 15:18—יְיָ יִמְלֹךְ לְעֹלָם וָעֶד; followed by the biblical verse Psalm 29:11—יְיָ עֹז לְעַמּוֹ יִתֵּן יְיָ יְבָרֵךְ אֶת עַמּוֹ בַשָּׁלוֹם. The verse Psalm 29:11 is also included at the end of the בִּרְכַּת הַמָּזוֹן, the Blessing after Meals.

The root מ־ל־ךְ appears as a perfect and imperfect verb, as well as a noun. The roots ב־ר־ךְ and נ־ת־ן also appear as imperfect verbs.

| strength | — | עֹז |

יְיָ מֶלֶךְ, יְיָ מָלָךְ, יְיָ יִמְלֹךְ לְעֹלָם וָעֶד. יְיָ עֹז לְעַמּוֹ יִתֵּן, יְיָ יְבָרֵךְ אֶת עַמּוֹ בַשָּׁלוֹם.

4. וְנֶאֱמַר (Zechariah 14:9)—This is the last line of the עָלֵינוּ prayer, quoting from the prophet Zechariah. The end of the עָלֵינוּ expresses a vision of a future time when the whole world will revere the Eternal One. The root ה־י־ה appears both as an imperfect verb and as a perfect verb with a reversing *vav*.

and it has been said (*verb from the root* א־מ־ר)	—	וְנֶאֱמַר
on that day	—	בַּיּוֹם הַהוּא
one	—	אֶחָד

וְנֶאֱמַר, וְהָיָה יְיָ לְמֶלֶךְ עַל כָּל הָאָרֶץ, בַּיּוֹם הַהוּא יִהְיֶה יְיָ אֶחָד, וּשְׁמוֹ אֶחָד:

5. Blessing for Sons (from Genesis 48:20) and Daughters—When the biblical patriarch Jacob is on his deathbed, his son Joseph brings his own two sons, Ephraim and Manasseh, to their grandfather for a blessing. The blessing said by Jewish parents to their sons on Shabbat and holidays comes from Jacob's words to his grandsons in Genesis 48:20. The parallel blessing for daughters is also included below.

may [he] make, let [him] make (*imperfect verb*)	—	יָשֵׂם
you (*feminine ending*)	—	ךְ

יְשִׂמְךָ אֱלֹהִים כְּאֶפְרַיִם וְכִמְנַשֶּׁה.
יְשִׂמֵךְ אֱלֹהִים כְּשָׂרָה רִבְקָה רָחֵל וְלֵאָה.

_____

_____

6. Genesis 2:1–3—This is the biblical account of the seventh day of Creation, the day of rest. This passage is included in the Shabbat evening service. Some chant this passage preceding the Shabbat evening קִדּוּשׁ, *Kiddush*, the blessing over wine.

and [they] were finished (*imperfect verb with reversing* vav)	—	וַיְכֻלּוּ
their array	—	צְבָאָם
and [he] finished (*imperfect verb with reversing* vav)	—	וַיְכַל
seventh	—	שְׁבִיעִי
work, labor	—	מְלָאכָה
imperfect verb with reversing vav *from the root* שׁ־ב־ת, *rest*	—	וַיִּשְׁבֹּת
imperfect verb with reversing vav *from the root* בּ־ר־ךּ, *bless*	—	וַיְבָרֶךְ
imperfect verb with reversing vav *from the root* קּ־ד־שׁ, *make holy*	—	וַיְקַדֵּשׁ
it (*direct object marker* אֵת *with* וֹ, *"him" or "it" ending*)	—	אֹתוֹ
because	—	כִּי

in it *(preposition* בְּ *with* וֹ, *"him" or "it" ending)*	—	בּוֹ
to do, to make *(from the root* עֹ־שֹׂ־ה)	—	לַעֲשׂוֹת

וַיְכֻלּוּ הַשָּׁמַיִם וְהָאָרֶץ וְכָל־צְבָאָם: ²וַיְכַל אֱלֹהִים בַּיּוֹם הַשְּׁבִיעִי
מְלַאכְתּוֹ אֲשֶׁר עָשָׂה וַיִּשְׁבֹּת בַּיּוֹם הַשְּׁבִיעִי מִכָּל־מְלַאכְתּוֹ
אֲשֶׁר עָשָׂה: ³וַיְבָרֶךְ אֱלֹהִים אֶת־יוֹם הַשְּׁבִיעִי וַיְקַדֵּשׁ אֹתוֹ, כִּי בוֹ
שָׁבַת מִכָּל־מְלַאכְתּוֹ אֲשֶׁר בָּרָא אֱלֹהִים לַעֲשׂוֹת:

_____

_____

_____

_____

_____

Translations

1. עֹשֶׂה שָׁלוֹם—Maker of peace in God's {His} heights, may God {He} make peace upon us and upon all Israel, and [all of you] say: Amen.

2. From אֲדוֹן עוֹלָם—And after the ending of all {everything}, alone awesome God {He} will reign. And God {He} was, and God {He} is, and God {He} will be, in splendor.

3. From the Torah Service (biblical phrases)—The Eternal is Ruler, the Eternal has ruled, the Eternal will rule {may the Eternal rule, let the Eternal rule} forever and ever. The Eternal will give {May the Eternal give, Let the Eternal give} strength to God's {His} people; the Eternal will bless {may the Eternal bless, let the Eternal bless} God's {His} people with peace.

4. וְנֶאֱמַר (Zechariah 14:9)—And it has been said, "The Eternal will be Sovereign over all the earth; on that day, the Eternal will be One and God's {His} name One."

5. Blessing for Sons {from Genesis 48:20} and Daughters—May God make you like Ephraim and like Manasseh. May God make you like Sarah, Rebekah, Rachel, and Leah.

6. Genesis 2:1–3—And the heavens and the earth were finished and all their array. And God finished on the seventh day God's {His} work that God {He} did {had done}. And God {He} rested on the seventh day from all God's {His} work that God {He} did {had done}. And God blessed the seventh day and made it holy, because in it God {He} rested from all God's {His} work that God created to do.

Exercises

1. Identify the root of each of the following verbs and whether it is a perfect, imperfect, or participle form.

Form	Root	Verb	Form	Root	Verb
_____	_____	יָצָא	_____	_____	נוֹתֵן
_____	_____	יִזְכֹּר	_____	_____	הָיָה
_____	_____	יֹאמַר	_____	_____	אָהַב
_____	_____	אוֹמֵר	_____	_____	יַעֲשֶׂה
_____	_____	יַעֲזֹר	_____	_____	יֹאכַל
_____	_____	בּוֹחֵר	_____	_____	יִהְיֶה
_____	_____	רָפָא	_____	_____	עָזַר
_____	_____	מָלַךְ	_____	_____	שׁוֹמֵר

2. Read and translate the following groups of sentences. Remember that the prefix *vav* can reverse the tense of a verb. Check your translations against those that follow.

a. הוּא אָמַר: "שָׁלוֹם עֲלֵיכֶם."
_____

וַיֹּאמֶר מֹשֶׁה: "עֲלֵיכֶם שָׁלוֹם."
_____

כָּל הָעָם יֹאמַר: "הַלְלוּיָהּ."
_____

אָנוּ אוֹמְרִים: "שַׁבָּת שָׁלוֹם."
_____

b. אַבְרָהָם אָכַל לֶחֶם בָּעֶרֶב.
_____

הָאֲמָהוֹת אוֹכְלוֹת בַּלַּיְלָה.
_____

יַעֲקֹב יֹאכַל פְּרִי בַּבֹּקֶר.
_____

וַיֹּאכַל יִצְחָק מַצָּה כָּל יוֹם.
_____

c. הָאָדוֹן זָכַר אֶת פְּנֵי עַבְדּוֹ.
_____

וַיִּזְכֹּר הָאָב אֶת פְּנֵי בְּנוֹ.
_____

אֲנַחְנוּ זוֹכְרִים אֶת פְּנֵי בְּנֵינוּ. _____

פְּנֵי הַבָּנִים קְדוֹשׁוֹת. _____

d. הַנָּבִיא שָׁמַע אֶת הָרוּחַ וְאֶת הַמַּיִם. _____

_____

וַיִּשְׁמַע הַנָּבִיא אֶת דְּבַר הָאֵל. _____

וַיִּשְׁמַע הָאָב וַיִּזְכֹּר אֶת דִּבְרֵי הַבְּרִית. _____

_____

הַבֵּן יִשְׁמַע אֶת הַדְּבָרִים וְהוּא יִזְכֹּר. _____

_____

e. הַמֶּלֶךְ יִבְחַר בְּמַלְאָךְ. _____

הַמַּלְאָךְ יֹאמַר דִּבְרֵי צֶדֶק. _____

מִי יִשְׁמַע אֶת הָאֱמֶת? _____

מִי יַעֲשֶׂה אֶת הַמִּצְוֹת? _____

f. בַּיּוֹם אֵין חֹשֶׁךְ וּבַלַּיְלָה אֵין אוֹר. _____

אֱלֹהִים בָּרָא אֶת הָאוֹר וְאֶת הַחֹשֶׁךְ. _____

_____

וַיִּבְרָא הָאֵל אֶת חַיֵּינוּ וְאֶת נַפְשׁוֹתֵינוּ. _____

_____

יִבְרָא הָאֵל רְפוּאָה לְכָל הַחוֹלִים. _____

_____

g. הָיָה שָׁלוֹם בֵּין יִשְׂרָאֵל וּבֵין מִצְרַיִם. _____

_____

יִהְיֶה שָׁלוֹם בֵּין כָּל הַגּוֹיִים. _____

וְהָיָה שָׁלוֹם בֵּין כָּל מִשְׁפְּחוֹת הָאֲדָמָה. _____

יְהִי שָׁלוֹם בָּעוֹלָם. _____

Translations

a. He said/did say/was saying/had said/has said: "Peace [be] upon you."

And Moses said/did say/was saying, "Upon you, peace."

All the nation/people will say/may say {May/Let all the nation/people say}: "Halleluyah."

We say/are saying/do say, "Shabbat shalom {a Sabbath of peace}."

b. Abraham ate/did eat/was eating/had eaten/has eaten bread in the evening.

The mothers are eating/do eat/eat in the night {at night}.

Jacob will/may eat {Let/May Jacob eat} a fruit in the morning.

Isaac ate/did eat/was eating/had eaten/has eaten matzah every day.

c. The lord/ruler remembered/did remember/was remembering/had remembered/has remembered the face of his slave/servant.

The father remembered/did remember/was remembering the face of his son/child.

We remember/are remembering/do remember the faces of our sons/children.

The faces of the sons/children are holy.

d. The prophet heard/did hear/was hearing/had heard/has heard the wind and the water.

The prophet heard/did hear/was hearing the word of God.

The father heard/did hear/was hearing and remembered/did remember/was remembering the words of the covenant.

The son/child will hear/may hear {Let/May the son/child hear} the words and he will/may remember {and let him/may he remember}.

e. The sovereign/king will/may choose {Let/May the sovereign/king choose} a messenger.

The messenger will/may say {Let/May the messenger say} words of justice/righteousness.

Who will/may hear the truth?

Who will/may do the mitzvot/commandments?

f. In the day {by day} there is no darkness and in the night {by night, at night} there is no light.

God created/did create/was creating/had created/has created the light and the darkness.

God created/did create/has created our lives and our souls.

God will/may create {May/Let God create} healing for all the sick.

g. [There] was/had been/has been peace {Peace was/had been/has been} between/among Israel and Egypt.

[There] will/may be peace {Let/May [there] be peace, Peace will/may be, Let/May peace be} between/among all the nations/peoples.

[There] will/may be peace {Let/May [there] be peace, Peace will/may be, Let/May peace be} between/among all the families of the earth.

May/Let [there] be peace {May/Let peace be} in the world.

Torah Study Text: Genesis 4:1–5, 8–10

The first three chapters of Genesis provide accounts of the creation of the world, the creation of the first man and woman, and their expulsion from the Garden of Eden. In the beginning of chapter 4, verses 1–10, the Torah presents the narrative of the first two brothers, Cain and Abel, and the first fratricide. In our Torah Study Text selection, verses 6 and 7, containing God's initial words to Cain, have been omitted from the passage in order to shorten it.

As with the last Torah Study Text, this passage contains many words, Hebrew roots, and grammatical concepts that have not yet been introduced. Read the Hebrew below to see how many of the words you can recognize. Underline or circle the words, roots, endings, and prefixes that you already know.

Genesis 4:1–5

וְהָאָדָם יָדַע אֶת־חַוָּה אִשְׁתּוֹ וַתַּהַר וַתֵּלֶד אֶת־קַיִן וַתֹּאמֶר קָנִיתִי אִישׁ אֶת־יְהוָֹה: ²וַתֹּסֶף לָלֶדֶת אֶת־אָחִיו אֶת־הָבֶל וַיְהִי־הֶבֶל רֹעֵה צֹאן וְקַיִן הָיָה עֹבֵד אֲדָמָה: ³וַיְהִי מִקֵּץ יָמִים וַיָּבֵא קַיִן מִפְּרִי הָאֲדָמָה מִנְחָה לַיהוָֹה: ⁴וְהֶבֶל הֵבִיא גַם־הוּא מִבְּכֹרוֹת צֹאנוֹ וּמֵחֶלְבֵהֶן וַיִּשַׁע יְהוָֹה אֶל־הֶבֶל וְאֶל־מִנְחָתוֹ: ⁵וְאֶל־קַיִן וְאֶל־מִנְחָתוֹ לֹא שָׁעָה וַיִּחַר לְקַיִן מְאֹד וַיִּפְּלוּ פָּנָיו:

Genesis 4:8–10

⁸וַיֹּאמֶר קַיִן אֶל־הֶבֶל אָחִיו וַיְהִי בִּהְיוֹתָם בַּשָּׂדֶה וַיָּקָם קַיִן אֶל־הֶבֶל אָחִיו וַיַּהַרְגֵהוּ: ⁹וַיֹּאמֶר יְהוָֹה אֶל־קַיִן אֵי הֶבֶל אָחִיךָ וַיֹּאמֶר לֹא יָדַעְתִּי הֲשֹׁמֵר אָחִי אָנֹכִי: ¹⁰וַיֹּאמֶר מֶה עָשִׂיתָ קוֹל דְּמֵי אָחִיךָ צֹעֲקִים אֵלַי מִן־הָאֲדָמָה:

Translating the Torah Study Text

Following is our Torah Study Text, Genesis 4:1–5 and 4:8–10, reprinted with a literal translation underneath each word. Using your knowledge of the building blocks of the Hebrew language and the meanings of the words provided below, translate this passage into clear English sentences. Write your translation on the lines following the text. This selection includes some grammatical forms and vocabulary that have not yet been introduced. You will need to rely, in part, on the translations provided.

Genesis 4:1–5

אֶת־קַיִן	וַתֵּלֶד	וַתַּהַר	אִשְׁתּוֹ	אֶת־חַוָּה	יָדַע	¹וְהָאָדָם
Kayin (Cain)	and she bore	and she conceived	his wife	Chava (Eve)	knew	and the man

לָלֶדֶת	²וַתֹּסֶף	יְהֹוָה:	אֶת־	אִישׁ	קָנִיתִי	וַתֹּאמֶר
to give birth/ to bear	she continued/ added/did again	the Eternal	with	man	I acquired	and she said

וְקַיִן	צֹאן	רֹעֵה	הֶבֶל	וַיְהִי־	אֶת־הֶבֶל	אֶת־אָחִיו
and Kayin (Cain)	flocks	shepherd	Hevel (Abel)	and [he] was/became	Hevel (Abel)	his brother

קַיִן	וַיָּבֵא	יָמִים	מִקֵּץ	³וַיְהִי	אֲדָמָה:	עֹבֵד	הָיָה
Kayin (Cain)	[he] brought	days	after	and it was/ happened	earth/ ground	work(er)	was

הוּא	גַם־	הֵבִיא	⁴וְהֶבֶל	לַיהֹוָה:	מִנְחָה	הָאֲדָמָה	מִפְּרִי
he	also	brought	and Hevel (Abel)	to the Eternal	offering/ gift	the earth/ground	from fruit

מִבְּכֹרוֹת	צֹאנוֹ	וּמֵחֶלְבֵהֶן	וַיִּשַׁע	יְהֹוָה	אֶל־
from firstborn	his flock	and from their fat/choicest part	and [he] turned to/gazed at	the Eternal	to/toward

הֶבֶל	וְאֶל־	מִנְחָתוֹ	⁵וְאֶל־	קַיִן	וְאֶל־	מִנְחָתוֹ:
Hevel (Abel)	and toward	his offering/gift	but toward	Kayin (Cain)	and toward	his offering/gift

לֹא	שָׁעָה	וַיִּחַר לְ	קַיִן	מְאֹד	וַיִּפְּלוּ	פָּנָיו:
not	turn to/gaze at	and was angry/distressed	Kayin (Cain)	very/exceedingly	and fell	his face

Genesis 4:8–10

⁸וַיֹּאמֶר	קַיִן	אֶל־	הֶבֶל	אָחִיו	וַיְהִי	בִּהְיוֹתָם	בַּשָּׂדֶה
and [he] said	Kayin (Cain)	to	Hevel (Abel)	his brother	and it was/happened	when they were	in the field

וַיָּקָם	קַיִן	אֶל־	הֶבֶל	אָחִיו	וַיַּהַרְגֵהוּ:	⁹וַיֹּאמֶר	יְהֹוָה
and arose	Kayin (Cain)	against	Hevel (Abel)	his brother	and he killed him	and [he] said	the Eternal

אֶל־	קַיִן	אֵי	הֶבֶל	אָחִיךָ	וַיֹּאמֶר	לֹא	יָדַעְתִּי	הֲשֹׁמֵר	אָחִי
to	Kayin (Cain)	where	Hevel (Abel)	your brother	and he said	not	I knew	guard/keeper	my brother

אָנֹכִי:	וַיֹּאמֶר ¹⁰	מֶה	עָשִׂיתָ	קוֹל	דְּמֵי	אָחִיךָ	צֹעֲקִים
I	and he said	what	you have done	voice/ sound	bloods of	your brother	cry out

אֵלַי	מִן־	הָאֲדָמָה:
to me	from	the earth/ground

Compare your translation of Genesis 4:1–5, 8–10 with the Torah translations below. Remember that verses 6 and 7, containing God's initial words to Cain, were omitted from our Torah Study Text in order to shorten the passage. They are, however, included in the English translations that follow.

¹Now the man knew his wife Eve, and she conceived and bore Cain, saying, "I have gained a male child with the help of the LORD." ²She then bore his brother Abel. Abel became a keeper of sheep, and Cain became a tiller of the soil. ³In the course of time, Cain brought an offering to the LORD from the fruit of the soil; ⁴and Abel, for his part, brought the choicest of the firstlings of his flock. The LORD paid heed to Abel and his offering, ⁵but to Cain and his offering He paid no heed. Cain was much distressed and his face fell. ⁶And the LORD said to Cain,

"Why are you distressed,

And why is your face fallen?

⁷Surely, if you do right,

There is uplift.

But if you do not do right

Sin crouches at the door;

Its urge is toward you,

Yet you can be its master."

⁸Cain said to his brother Abel…and when they were in the field, Cain set upon his brother Abel and killed him. ⁹The LORD said to Cain, "Where is your brother Abel?" And he said, "I do not know. Am I my brother's keeper?" ¹⁰Then He said, "What have you done? Hark, your brother's blood cries out to Me from the ground!"

JPS HEBREW-ENGLISH TANAKH: THE TRADITIONAL HEBREW TEXT AND THE NEW JPS TRANSLATION—2D ED. PHILADELPHIA: THE JEWISH PUBLICATION SOCIETY, **1999.**

CHAPTER 3

¹Now the man had known his wife Eve, and she conceived and bore Cain, saying, "I have acquired a man with HASHEM." ²And additionally she bore his brother Abel. Abel became a shepherd, and Cain became a tiller of the ground.

³After a period of time, Cain brought an offering to HASHEM of the fruit of the ground; ⁴and as for Abel, he also brought of the firstlings of his flock and from their choicest. HASHEM turned to Abel and his offering, ⁵but to Cain and to his offering He did not turn. This annoyed Cain exceedingly, and his countenance fell.

⁶And HASHEM said to Cain, "Why are you annoyed, and why has your countenance fallen? ⁷Surely, if you improve yourself, you will be forgiven. But if you do not improve yourself, sin rests at the door. Its desire is toward you, yet you can conquer it."

⁸Cain spoke with his brother Abel. And it happened when they were in the field, that Cain rose up against his brother Abel and killed him.

⁹HASHEM said to Cain, "Where is Abel your brother?"

And he said, "I do not know. Am I my brother's keeper?"

¹⁰Then He said, "What have you done? The blood of your brother cries out to Me from the ground!"

THE CHUMASH, ARTSCROLL SERIES, STONE EDITION. BROOKLYN: MESORAH PUBLICATIONS, 1993.

¹The human knew Havva his wife,
she became pregnant and bore Kayin.
She said:
Kaniti/I-have-gotten
a man, as has YHWH!
²She continued bearing—his brother, Hevel.
Now Hevel became a shepherd of flocks, and Kayin became a worker of the soil.

³It was, after the passing of days
that Kayin brought, from the fruit of the soil, a gift to YHWH,
⁴and as for Hevel, he too brought—from the firstborn of his flock, from their fat-parts.
YHWH had regard for Hevel and his gift,
⁵for Kayin and his gift he had no regard.
Kayin became exceedingly upset and his face fell.

⁶YHWH said to Kayin:
Why are you so upset? Why has your face fallen?
⁷Is it not thus:
If you intend good, bear-it-aloft,

but if you do not intend good,
at the entrance is sin, a crouching-demon,
toward you his lust—
but you can rule over him.

⁸Kayin said to Hevel his brother...
But then it was, when they were out in the field
that Kayin rose up against Hevel his brother
and he killed him.
⁹YHWH said to Kayin:
Where is Hevel your brother?
He said:
I do not know. Am I the watcher of my brother?
¹⁰Now he said:
What have you done!
A sound—your brother's blood cries out to me from the soil!

THE FIVE BOOKS OF MOSES: A NEW TRANSLATION WITH INTRODUCTIONS, COMMENTARY, AND NOTES BY EVERETT FOX. NEW YORK: SCHOCKEN BOOKS, 1995.

And the man knew Havva his wife; and she conceived, and bore Qayin saying, I have acquired a manchild from the LORD. And she again bore, his brother Hevel. And Hevel was a keeper of sheep, but Qayin was a tiller of the ground. And in process of time it came to pass, that Qayin brought of the fruit of the ground an offering to the LORD. And Hevel, he also brought of the firstlings of his flock and of the fat parts thereof. And the LORD had respect to Hevel and to his offering: but to Qayin and to his offering he had not respect. And Qayin was very angry, and his face fell. And the LORD said to Qayin, Why art thou angry? and why art thou crestfallen? If thou doest well, shalt thou not be accepted? and if thou doest not well, sin crouches at the door, and to thee shall be his desire. Yet thou mayst rule over him. And Qayin talked with Hevel his brother: and it came to pass, when they were in the field, that Qayin rose up against Hevel his brother, and slew him. And the LORD said to Qayin, Where is Hevel thy brother? And he said, I know not: am I my brother's keeper? And he said, What hast thou done? the voice of thy brother's blood cries to me from the ground.

THE JERUSALEM BIBLE, PUBLISHED FOR THE NAHUM ZEEV WILLIAMS FAMILY FOUNDATION AT HECHAL SHLOMO, JERUSALEM. JERUSALEM: KOREN PUBLISHERS JERUSALEM LTD., 1969.

Vocabulary

Locate each of the following words in the Torah Study Text: Genesis 4:1–5, 8–10.

human being, man, humankind *m*	—	אָדָם
woman, wife *f*	—	אִשָּׁה
man *m*	—	אִישׁ
brother *m*	—	אָח
to, toward	—	אֶל
no, not	—	לֹא
sound, voice *m*	—	קוֹל
blood *m*	—	דָּם

Notes on the Vocabulary

1. The Hebrew word אָדָם can mean either "human being" (male or female, as in Genesis 1:27) or "humankind." When it refers to a single male human being, such as the first *adam*, it can be translated as "man." It has also become the male name "Adam." The word אִישׁ means "man" as opposed to אִשָּׁה, "woman."
2. The word אִישׁ has an irregular plural form, אֲנָשִׁים, which can be translated as "men" or "people." The word אִשָּׁה has an irregular plural form, נָשִׁים, "women," and an irregular word pair form, אֵשֶׁת, meaning "woman of/wife of." All these forms are included in the glossary.
3. Hebrew prepositions, such as the word אֶל, do not always translate consistently into English. (For example, in verse 8 of our Torah Study Text, Cain rises up אֶל, "against," Abel.)
4. דָּם, "blood," is the first of the Ten Plagues of the Exodus story, enumerated at the Passover seder.

The basic meaning of the root י־ד־ע is "know." This root follows the ▦וֹ▦ participle pattern, with a slight variation in vowels caused by the final root letter ע. The following are the four participle forms:

f pl יוֹדְעוֹת   *m pl* יוֹדְעִים   *f sg* יוֹדַעַת   *m sg* יוֹדֵעַ

The root י־ד־ע appears twice in this chapter's Torah Study Text:

(verse 1)

And the man knew Chava his	—	וְהָאָדָם יָדַע אֶת־חַוָּה
wife and she conceived		אִשְׁתּוֹ וַתַּהַר

(verse 9)

And he said: I knew not — וַיֹּאמֶר לֹא יָדַעְתִּי

As verse 1 illustrates, the root יָדַע can imply having sexual relations.

The following words, both ancient and modern, are derived from the root יָדַע. The root letter י drops out in some words formed from this root.

knowledge, view, opinion	—	דֵּעָה
knowledge, discernment, understanding	—	דַּעַת
in the Bible: knowledge, thought; *in modern Hebrew:* science	—	מַדָּע
scientific	—	מַדָּעִי
scientist	—	מַדְעָן
known, certain	—	יָדוּעַ
knowledge, news, information	—	יְדִיעָה
latest news *(name of an Israeli newspaper)*	—	יְדִיעוֹת אַחֲרוֹנוֹת
bulletin	—	יְדִיעוֹן
herald, informant, announcer, correspondent	—	מוֹדִיעַ
information, intelligence (*as in* "military intelligence")	—	מוֹדִיעִין
in the Bible: kinsman; *in modern Hebrew:* acquaintance, friend	—	מוֹדָע
conscious, conscious mind	—	מוּדָע
notice, announcement, advertisement	—	מוֹדָעָה

The basic meaning of the root עָבַד is "work" or "serve." Words relating to both labor and to religious service are derived from this root.

slave, servant	—	עֶבֶד
work, labor; service, worship	—	עֲבוֹדָה
prayer {worship that is in the heart}	—	עֲבוֹדָה שֶׁבַּלֵּב

idol worship, idolatry {alien worship} —	עֲבוֹדָה זָרָה
servitude, bondage —	עַבְדוּת
Obadiah ("servant of God," *name of a prophet*) —	עֹבַדְיָה
workable —	עָבִיד
employer —	מַעֲבִיד
laboratory —	מַעְבָּדָה

The root עׂ-בׂ-ד follows the ▦ ▦ו▦ participle pattern. The following are the four participle forms:

m sg עוֹבֵד   *f sg* עוֹבֶדֶת   *m pl* עוֹבְדִים   *f pl* עוֹבְדוֹת

The root עׂ-בׂ-ד appears once in our Torah Study Text:

(verse 2)

and Cain was a worker of the earth/ground —	וְקַיִן הָיָה עֹבֵד אֲדָמָה

Building Blocks

More on the Reversing *Vav*

The reversing *vav* is generally used in biblical Hebrew to indicate sequential, continuing action. A string of verbs with reversing *vav*s indicates a series of actions that occur one after the other. The verbs in the following example, from verse 1, are feminine forms that will be introduced in the next chapter.

And she conceived and she bore Cain and she said —	וַתַּהַר וַתֵּלֶד אֶת־קַיִן וַתֹּאמֶר

Hence, it is possible to translate the reversing *vav* using other words besides "and" that indicate sequential action, such as "then" or "now" or "so."

The absence of a reversing *vav* in a passage can have a subtle nuance. If there is a verb without a reversing *vav* among a string of verbs with reversing *vav*s, it implies an action that is not part of the narrative sequence, but is a kind of aside or parenthetical statement providing additional background information. For an example of this, see the Torah Commentary on verse 1 below.

The Preposition אֵת

In Chapter 4 of *Aleph Isn't Enough*, we introduced the word אֵת as the untranslatable direct object marker. The word אֵת (or אֶת) is also used as a preposition meaning "with." It is used as a preposition much less frequently than as the direct object marker. Such usage does, however, appear in our Torah Study Text in verse 1:

She said: I have acquired a	וַתֹּאמֶר קָנִיתִי אִישׁ אֶת־
man with the Eternal. —	יְהוָֹה:

This usage of the word אֵת is the basis of the second Torah Commentary cited below.

Verse 1 does not begin וַיֵּדַע הָאָדָם, with a reversing *vav*. Instead, it uses a verb without a reversing *vav*: וְהָאָדָם יָדַע, implying that this action is background information and not part of the continuing narrative sequence: "The man had known {had sexual relations with} his wife."

Thus, Rashi asserts that sexual relations, pregnancy, and childbirth were part of the couple's prior life in the Garden of Eden, a view in opposition to the notion that sexuality only entered the world as a result of Adam and Eve's sin and expulsion from the Garden.

וְהָאָדָם יָדַע. *[The man had sexual relations with his wife] already, before the matter related above, before he sinned and was driven out of the Garden of Eden. And so too, the pregnancy and the birth. For if it was written:* וַיֵּדַע הָאָדָם, *it would imply that after he was driven out, he had children.*

RASHI ON GENESIS 4:1

The Torah only records the birth of sons to Adam and Eve, but how could the human race have continued without the birth of daughters? If, in the following excerpts from verses 1 and 2, the word אֵת is regarded as the preposition "with," then it implies that other children, possibly daughters, were also born: וַתֵּלֶד אֶת־קַיִן "and she gave birth with Cain"; וַתֹּסֶף לָלֶדֶת אֶת־אָחִיו אֶת־הָבֶל, "and she added/increased to give birth with his brother, with Abel."

וַתַּהַר וַתֵּלֶד אֶת־קַיִן, *and she conceived and she bore* אֵת *(with) Cain. Rabbi Yehoshua ben Korchah said: Two people went into the bed and seven came out of it: Cain and his twin sister, Abel and his two twin sisters.*

B'REISHIT RABBAH 22:3

In verse 10, the plural word-pair form דְּמֵי, "bloods of," appears, instead of the singular דַּם, "blood (of)."

Rabbi Yudan said: דַּם אָחִיךָ, *"the blood of your brother," is not written here, but*

דְּמֵי אָחִיךָ, *"the bloods of your brother"—his blood and the blood of his descendants.*

B'REISHIT RABBAH 22:21

The idea that a killer kills not only the victim, but also all the unborn potential offspring of that victim, is also stated in the Talmud. In the following passage, the witnesses in a capital case are warned to give careful testimony, because the life of the accused as well as the lives of all possible future offspring are at stake.

How did they admonish the witnesses in capital cases? They brought them in and admonished them,... "You must know that capital cases are not like monetary cases. In cases concerning property, a person may pay money and make atonement, but in capital cases, the witness is answerable for the blood of the one [who is wrongly condemned] and the blood of [that person's potential] descendants to the end of the world. For thus we find with Cain, who killed his brother, as it is written: דְּמֵי אָחִיךָ צוֹעֲקִים, *"the bloods of your brother cry out." It does not say:* דַּם אָחִיךָ, *"the blood of your brother," but* דְּמֵי אָחִיךָ, *"the bloods of your brother," his blood and the blood of his descendants.... Therefore a single person was created alone, to teach you that anyone who destroys a single soul, Scripture accounts it as if having destroyed an entire world. And whoever saves a single soul, Scripture accounts it as if having saved an entire world.*

MISHNAH SANHEDRIN 4:5; BT SANHEDRIN 37A

Exercises

1. Make flash cards for each of the new vocabulary words and Hebrew roots introduced in this chapter, or use the flash card set published as a companion to this book. Review the cards to learn all of them.

2. Draw a line connecting each Hebrew word to its English translation. For some words, there can be more than one correct translation.

not   אִשָּׁה

man

wife   אֶל

sound   אִישׁ

to

woman   קוֹל

no   דָּם

human being

brother   אָדָם

voice   לֹא

toward

blood   אָח

3. The following are singular and plural forms of nouns introduced as vocabulary in this chapter. Both אִישׁ and אִשָּׁה have irregular plural forms, listed here and in the Glossary. Draw a line connecting each plural noun to its singular form. Translate both into English.

_____	נָשִׁים	אִישׁ	_____
_____	אָחִים	דָּם	_____
_____	אֲנָשִׁים	אִשָּׁה	_____
_____	דָּמִים	קוֹל	_____
_____	קוֹלוֹת	אָח	_____

4. Read and translate the following groups of words.

.b
_____	קוֹל מַיִם
_____	קוֹל הָעָם
_____	קוֹל שׁוֹפָר
_____	קוֹל אָדָם
_____	רוּחַ אָדָם

.a
_____	נִשְׁמַת אָדָם
_____	דִּבְרֵי אָדָם
_____	דַּם הָאָדָם
_____	יַד אָדָם
_____	מַעֲשֵׂה יְדֵי אָדָם

.d
_____	אָח גָּדוֹל
_____	קוֹל אָחִיךָ
_____	אִישׁ אֶל אָחִיו
_____	בְּרִית אַחִים
_____	שְׁלוֹם אֲחֵיכֶם

.c
_____	כָּל אִישׁ
_____	אִישׁ גִּבּוֹר
_____	אִישׁ חֶסֶד
_____	אַנְשֵׁי אֱמֶת
_____	אֲנָשִׁים וְנָשִׁים

.f
_____	דַּם אֲנָשִׁים
_____	דַּם עֲבָדִים
_____	דַּם הַפָּנִים
_____	פָּנִים אֶל פָּנִים
_____	לֹא אֶל הַבַּיִת

.e
_____	לֵב אִשָּׁה
_____	דֶּרֶךְ אִשָּׁה
_____	אִשְׁתְּךָ
_____	אֵשֶׁת בְּנוֹ
_____	נְשֵׁי הַמֶּלֶךְ

5. Identify the root of each of the following participles and whether the participle form is masculine or feminine, singular or plural. Translate the meaning of the root.

m/f	sing/pl	Translation	Root	Participle
_____	_____	_____	_____	מְקַדֵּשׁ
_____	_____	_____	_____	עוֹבֵד
_____	_____	_____	_____	נוֹתְנִים
_____	_____	_____	_____	יוֹדְעִים
_____	_____	_____	_____	מְצַוֶּה

				יוֹדֵעַ
				אוֹמֶרֶת
				עוֹבְדוֹת
				שׁוֹמֵעַ
				אוֹכְלִים

EXTRA CREDIT

A Modern Poem with a Biblical Theme

Modern Hebrew writers have a rich 3,000-year literary tradition upon which to draw in their work. Biblical phrases, fragments of texts, and allusions to familiar stories all find their way into contemporary Hebrew poetry, illuminating contemporary concerns. An excellent example is provided by the following poem, written by the Israeli poet Dan Pagis.

Dan Pagis was born in 1930 in Bukovina. He spent several years in a concentration camp during World War II and came to Israel (then Palestine) in 1946. The biblical narrative of fratricide in Genesis 4 provides the backdrop to the following Holocaust poem by Pagis:

Written in pencil in the sealed freight car   כָּתוּב בְּעִפָּרוֹן בַּקָּרוֹן הֶחָתוּם

Here in this transport   כָּאן בַּמִּשְׁלוֹחַ הַזֶּה

am I, Eve,   אֲנִי חַוָּה

with Abel, my son.   עִם הֶבֶל בְּנִי

If you see my older son   אִם תִּרְאוּ אֶת בְּנִי הַגָּדוֹל

Cain son of Adam [or: Cain, human being],   קַיִן בֶּן אָדָם

tell him that I   תַּגִּידוּ לוֹ שֶׁאֲנִי

Torah Study Text: Vocabulary and Root Review

This unit's Torah Study Text, Genesis 4:1–5, 8–10, is reprinted below, highlighting the new vocabulary words as well as the words formed from the new Hebrew roots introduced in Chapter 3. Read this passage again, recalling the meaning of each of the highlighted words or roots.

Genesis 4:1–5

‎¹וְהָאָדָם **יָדַע** אֶת־חַוָּה **אִשְׁתּוֹ** וַתַּהַר וַתֵּלֶד אֶת־קַיִן וַתֹּאמֶר קָנִיתִי **אִישׁ** אֶת־יְהֹוָה: ²וַתֹּסֶף לָלֶדֶת אֶת־**אָחִיו** אֶת־הָבֶל וַיְהִי־הֶבֶל רֹעֵה צֹאן וְקַיִן הָיָה **עֹבֵד** אֲדָמָה: ³וַיְהִי מִקֵּץ יָמִים וַיָּבֵא קַיִן מִפְּרִי הָאֲדָמָה מִנְחָה לַיהֹוָה: ⁴וְהֶבֶל הֵבִיא גַם־הוּא מִבְּכֹרוֹת צֹאנוֹ וּמֵחֶלְבֵהֶן וַיִּשַׁע יְהֹוָה **אֶל**־הֶבֶל וְ**אֶל**־מִנְחָתוֹ: ⁵וְ**אֶל**־קַיִן וְ**אֶל**־מִנְחָתוֹ **לֹא** שָׁעָה וַיִּחַר לְקַיִן מְאֹד וַיִּפְּלוּ פָנָיו:

Genesis 4:8–10

‎⁸וַיֹּאמֶר קַיִן **אֶל**־הֶבֶל **אָחִיו** וַיְהִי בִּהְיוֹתָם בַּשָּׂדֶה וַיָּקָם קַיִן **אֶל**־הֶבֶל **אָחִיו** וַיַּהַרְגֵהוּ: ⁹וַיֹּאמֶר יְהֹוָה **אֶל**־קַיִן אֵי הֶבֶל **אָחִיךָ** וַיֹּאמֶר **לֹא** **יָדַעְתִּי** הֲשֹׁמֵר **אָחִי** אָנֹכִי: ¹⁰וַיֹּאמֶר מֶה עָשִׂיתָ **קוֹל** דְּמֵי **אָחִיךָ** צֹעֲקִים אֵלַי מִן־הָאֲדָמָה:

Building Blocks

Feminine Verb Forms

There are many different verb patterns in Hebrew. In Unit 1, Chapter 2, we introduced masculine הוּא ("he" or "it") forms of the simplest Hebrew verb pattern.

In this chapter we introduce the corresponding feminine הִיא ("she" or "it") forms.

Perfect Verbs

The feminine הִיא ("she" or "it") perfect form corresponding to the masculine ◼ ◻ ◼ ◻ is as follows:

הָ◼ ְ◼ ָ

Examples:

[he] said	—	אָמַר	**[he] worked**	—	עָבַד
[she] said	—	אָמְרָה	**[she] worked**	—	עָבְדָה

Remember that perfect verbs describe action that has been completed and can be translated in several different ways. For example, עָבְדָה could be translated as "she worked," "she did work," "she was working," "she had worked," or "she has worked."

Imperfect Verbs

The feminine הִיא ("she" or "it") imperfect form corresponding to the masculine ◼ ◼ ◼ י is as follows:

ת ◼ ◼ ◼

Examples:

[he] will/may say	—	יֹאמַר	**[he] will/may work**	—	יַעֲבֹד
[she] will/may say	—	תֹּאמַר	**[she] will/may work**	—	תַּעֲבֹד

Remember that imperfect verbs can indicate the future tense, ongoing incompleted action, or action that is wished or urged. So, for example, תַּעֲבֹד could be translated as "she will work," "she may work," "may she work," or "let her work."

The Question הַ

In Chapter 1 of *Aleph Isn't Enough*, we introduced the prefix הַ meaning "the." In the vast majority of cases, the prefix הַ has this meaning. But occasionally, the prefix הַ is used, like a question mark in English, to indicate that a sentence is a question. An example of this question הַ appears in our Torah Study Text, verse 9:

the guard/keeper of my brother *or* my brother's guard/keeper	—	שֹׁמֵר אָחִי
My brother's guard/keeper am I? *or* Am I my brother's guard/keeper?	—	הֲשֹׁמֵר אָחִי אָנֹכִי

Torah Study Text with Building Blocks

Following are excerpts from this unit's Torah Study Text, Genesis 4:1–2 and Genesis 4:9, reprinted with the new Building Blocks highlighted. Reread these verses, noting the appearance of feminine imperfect verbs with the reversing *vav* and the use of the question הַ. A translation is provided below for only the highlighted Building Blocks. Remember that there could be other possible translations. For a full translation of the verses, refer back to Chapter 3.

Genesis 4:1–2

¹וְהָאָדָם יָדַע אֶת־חַוָּה אִשְׁתּוֹ **וַתַּהַר וַתֵּלֶד** אֶת־קַיִן **וַתֹּאמֶר** קָנִיתִי אִישׁ אֶת־יְהוָה: ²**וַתֹּסֶף** לָלֶדֶת אֶת־אָחִיו אֶת־הֶבֶל וַיְהִי־הֶבֶל רֹעֵה צֹאן וְקַיִן הָיָה עֹבֵד אֲדָמָה:

Genesis 4:9

⁹וַיֹּאמֶר יְהוָֹה אֶל־קַיִן אֵי הֶבֶל אָחִיךָ וַיֹּאמֶר לֹא יָדַעְתִּי **הֲשֹׁמֵר אָחִי אָנֹכִי**:

[and she] conceived	—	וַתַּהַר
[and she] bore	—	וַתֵּלֶד
[and she] said	—	וַתֹּאמֶר
[and she] continued/added/did again	—	וַתֹּסֶף
Am I my brother's keeper?	—	הֲשֹׁמֵר אָחִי אָנֹכִי

הִיא Forms

The following chart includes the feminine הִיא ("she" or "it") participle, perfect, and imperfect forms for every root introduced thus far that follows the simple pattern. This chart present the regular vowels for each form, but alternate or irregular vowels sometimes appear in biblical texts. Keep in mind that this chart is included for enrichment only. It is not necessary to memorize these forms.

It may be helpful to notice certain variations:
• In roots that end with the letter ה, such as ה־י־ה and ע־שׂ־ה, the root letter ה becomes a ת in the feminine perfect form: עָשְׂתָה, הָיְתָה.
• In many roots that begin with the letter י or the letter נ, such as י־צ־א, י־ד־ע, and נ־ת־ן, that first root letter י or נ drops out in the imperfect form: תִּתֵּן, תֵּצֵא, תֵּדַע. This happens with the masculine imperfect forms too: יִתֵּן, יֵצֵא, יֵדַע.

	Imperfect	Perfect	Participle	Root	
	תֶּאֱהַב	אָהֲבָה	אוֹהֶבֶת	א־ה־ב	love
	תֹּאכַל	אָכְלָה	אוֹכֶלֶת	א־כ־ל	eat
	תֹּאמַר	אָמְרָה	אוֹמֶרֶת	א־מ־ר	say
	תִּבְחַר	בָּחֲרָה	בּוֹחֶרֶת	ב־ח־ר	choose
	תִּבְרָא	בָּרְאָה	בּוֹרֵאת	ב־ר־א	create
	תִּהְיֶה	הָיְתָה	–	ה־י־ה	be
	תִּזְכֹּר	זָכְרָה	זוֹכֶרֶת	ז־כ־ר	remember
(irregular imperfect—root letter י missing)	תֵּדַע	יָדְעָה	יוֹדַעַת	י־ד־ע	know
	תֵּצֵא	יָצְאָה	יוֹצֵאת	י־צ־א	go out
	תִּמְלֹךְ	מָלְכָה	מוֹלֶכֶת	מ־ל־ך	rule
(irregular imperfect—root letter נ missing)	תִּתֵּן	נָתְנָה	נוֹתֶנֶת	נ־ת־ן	give
	תַּעֲבֹד	עָבְדָה	עוֹבֶדֶת	ע־ב־ד	work, serve
	תַּעֲזֹר	עָזְרָה	עוֹזֶרֶת	ע־ז־ר	help
	תַּעֲשֶׂה	עָשְׂתָה	עוֹשָׂה	ע־שׂ־ה	make, do
	תִּרְפָּא	רָפְאָה	רוֹפֵאת	ר־פ־א	heal
	תִּשְׁמַע	שָׁמְעָה	שׁוֹמַעַת	שׁ־מ־ע	hear
	תִּשְׁמֹר	שָׁמְרָה	שׁוֹמֶרֶת	שׁ־מ־ר	guard, keep

Additional Reading and Translation Practice

Translate the following Hebrew excerpts, using the extra vocabulary words provided. Check your translations against the English translations that follow.

1. From Genesis 1:2—This is the beginning of the second verse in Unit One's Torah Study Text. The word אֶרֶץ is grammatically feminine; hence it is followed by the feminine perfect form of the root ה־י־ה.

void and nothingness	—	תֹהוּ וָבֹהוּ
[the] deep	—	תְהוֹם

וְהָאָרֶץ הָיְתָה תֹהוּ וָבֹהוּ וְחֹשֶׁךְ עַל־פְּנֵי תְהוֹם

_____

_____

2. Psalm 150:6—This is the last line of the last psalm in the Book of Psalms. This psalm is included in the morning service. The word נְשָׁמָה is grammatically feminine; hence the root ה־ל־ל appears in a feminine imperfect form. Remember that there is more than one way to translate imperfect verbs.

Yah (a name for God, the first two letters of the four-letter Divine Name)	—	יָה

כֹּל הַנְּשָׁמָה תְהַלֵּל יָה הַלְלוּ־יָהּ:

_____

_____

3. From נִשְׁמַת כָּל חַי—This prayer is included in the Shabbat morning service. Feminine imperfect verbs (including one from the root ב־ר־ךְ) are used because the words נְשָׁמָה and רוּחַ are feminine.

living	—	חַי
flesh	—	בָּשָׂר
feminine imperfect verb from the root פ־א־ר, glorify	—	תְּפָאֵר
feminine imperfect verb from the root ר־ו־ם, raise up, exalt	—	תְּרוֹמֵם

remembrance	—	זֵכֶר
always, continually	—	תָּמִיד
until, unto	—	עַד

נִשְׁמַת כָּל חַי תְּבָרֵךְ אֶת שִׁמְךָ, יְיָ אֱלֹהֵינוּ, וְרוּחַ כָּל בָּשָׂר תְּפָאֵר
וּתְרוֹמֵם זִכְרְךָ, מַלְכֵּנוּ, תָּמִיד. מִן הָעוֹלָם וְעַד הָעוֹלָם אַתָּה אֵל...

_____

_____

4. From הַתִּקְוָה—"Hatikvah" is the national anthem of the State of Israel. Below is the second half of "Hatikvah." The word תִּקְוָה is grammatically feminine.

still, yet	—	עוֹד
feminine perfect verb from the root אָ־בַ־ד, be lost, perish	—	אָבְדָה
hope	—	תִּקְוָה
two thousand years	—	שְׁנוֹת אַלְפַּיִם
to be (*from the root* הָ־יָ־ד)	—	לִהְיוֹת
free	—	חָפְשִׁי

עוֹד לֹא אָבְדָה תִּקְוָתֵנוּ, הַתִּקְוָה שְׁנוֹת אַלְפַּיִם,
לִהְיוֹת עַם חָפְשִׁי בְּאַרְצֵנוּ, בְּאֶרֶץ צִיּוֹן וִירוּשָׁלַיִם.

_____

_____

5. From Genesis 3:6—Eating the forbidden fruit in the Garden of Eden led to Adam and Eve's expulsion from the Garden.

feminine imperfect verb with reversing vav from the root רָ־אָ־ד, see	—	וַתֵּרֶא
that	—	כִּי
tree	—	עֵץ
food, eating	—	מַאֲכָל

feminine imperfect verb with reversing vav from the root לֹ־קֹ־חַ, take	—	וַתִּקַּח
feminine imperfect verb with reversing vav from the root נֹ־תֹ־ן, give	—	וַתִּתֵּן
also, too	—	גַּם
with	—	עִם

וַתֵּרֶא הָאִשָּׁה כִּי טוֹב הָעֵץ לְמַאֲכָל...וַתִּקַּח מִפִּרְיוֹ וַתֹּאכַל
וַתִּתֵּן גַּם־לְאִישָׁהּ עִמָּהּ וַיֹּאכַל:

_____

_____

6. From Proverbs 6:20, 22, 23—The words מִצְוָה and תּוֹרָה are both grammatically feminine. It is not clear which of the two is the subject of verse 22.

guard, keep *(command form)*	—	נְצֹר
my son, my child (בֵּן *with* יָ , "my" ending)	—	בְּנִי
don't abandon	—	אַל־תִּטֹּשׁ
when you walk about {in your walking about}	—	בְּהִתְהַלֶּכְךָ
feminine imperfect verb from the root נֹ־חֹ־ה, guide	—	תַּנְחֶה
you (אֵת *with* ךְ , "you" ending)	—	אֹתָךְ
when you lie down {in your lying down}	—	בְּשָׁכְבְּךָ
for, because	—	כִּי

²⁰נְצֹר בְּנִי מִצְוַת אָבִיךָ, וְאַל־תִּטֹּשׁ תּוֹרַת אִמֶּךָ:
²²בְּהִתְהַלֶּכְךָ תַּנְחֶה אֹתָךְ בְּשָׁכְבְּךָ תִּשְׁמֹר עָלֶיךָ...
²³כִּי נֵר מִצְוָה וְתוֹרָה אוֹר...

_____

_____

_____

Translations

1. From Genesis 1:2—And the earth was void and nothingness and darkness [was] on [the] face {surface} of [the] deep.

2. Psalm 150:6—Every living being {all the breath} will praise *Yah*. Hallelujah. *or* Let every living being {all the breath} praise *Yah*.

3. From נִשְׁמַת כָּל חַי—The soul/breath of all living will bless Your name, Eternal our God, and [the] spirit of all flesh will glorify and exalt Your remembrance, our Sovereign, continually. From eternity and unto eternity You are God... *or* May the soul/breath of all living bless Your name....may the spirit of all flesh glorify and exalt Your remembrance....

4. From הַתִּקְוָה—Still is not lost/has not perished our hope {Our hope is still not lost/has not perished}, the hope [for] two thousand years, to be a free people in our land, in the land of Zion and Jerusalem.

5. From Genesis 3:6—The woman saw that good is the tree for food/eating...so she took from its fruit and she ate and she gave also to her man with her and he ate.

6. From Proverbs 6:20, 22, 23—[20]Keep, my child, the commandment of your father and don't abandon the Torah {teaching} of your mother. / [22]When you walk about, it will guide {may it guide} you; when you lie down, it will guard {may it guard} over you.... / [23]For a lamp/light is mitzvah {commandment} and Torah is light....

Exercises

1. Draw a line connecting each of the following feminine verb forms with the corresponding masculine verb form. Identify the root and whether the forms are perfect, imperfect, or participles.

Form	Root	Masculine	Feminine
_____	_____	יוֹדֵעַ	יָדְעָה
_____	_____	אָמַר	עָבְדָה
_____	_____	יַעֲבֹד	תִּהְיֶה
_____	_____	בּוֹרֵא	יוֹדַעַת
_____	_____	יָדַע	תֹּאמַר
_____	_____	יֹאכַל	בּוֹרֵאת
_____	_____	עוֹבֵד	בָּחֲרָה
_____	_____	יִהְיֶה	תַּעֲבֹד
_____	_____	עָבַד	עוֹבֶדֶת
_____	_____	יֹאמַר	אָמְרָה
_____	_____	בָּחַר	תֹּאכַל

2. Read and translate the following groups of sentences. Remember that the prefix *vav* can reverse the tense of a verb. Check your translations against those that follow.

a. וַיִּשְׁמַע יַעֲקֹב אֶת קוֹל אִשְׁתּוֹ.

_____

וַתִּשְׁמַע רָחֵל אֶת קוֹל בָּנֶיהָ.

_____

הָאִישׁ שָׁמַע אֶת קוֹל הָרוּחַ.

_____

הָאִשָּׁה שָׁמְעָה אֶת קוֹל הַשּׁוֹפָר.

_____

b. אַתָּה אוֹהֵב אֶת אִשְׁתְּךָ בְּכָל נַפְשְׁךָ.

_____

וַתֶּאֱהַב רִבְקָה אֶת אִישָׁהּ בְּכָל לִבָּהּ.

_____

אֲנַחְנוּ אוֹהֲבִים אֶת נָשֵׁינוּ בְּכָל נַפְשׁוֹתֵינוּ.

_____

יִצְחָק יֶאֱהַב אֶת אִשְׁתּוֹ כָּל חַיָּיו.

_____

c. הַמִּשְׁפָּחָה זָכְרָה אֶת דַּם הַחוֹלִים.

_____

וַתִּזְכֹּר הַחוֹלָה אֶת פְּנֵי מִשְׁפַּחְתָּהּ.

_____

מִי יִזְכֹּר אֶת דַּם חוֹלֵינוּ? מִי יַעֲזֹר לָנוּ?

_____

אַתָּה עוֹזֵר לְחוֹלֵי מִשְׁפַּחְתְּךָ.

_____

d. עֶבֶד הַמֶּלֶךְ עָשָׂה מַעֲשִׂים גְּבוֹרִים.

_____

וַיַּעַשׂ הָעֶבֶד מַעֲשֵׂי חֶסֶד.

_____

וַיַּעֲבֹד הָעֶבֶד מִן הַבֹּקֶר כָּל הַיּוֹם.

_____

וּבָעֶרֶב הוּא לֹא עָבַד וְלֹא יָצָא מִבֵּיתוֹ.

_____

e. בֵּית הַנָּבִיא הָיָה בֵּין הַדֶּרֶךְ וְהַמַּיִם.

_____

וַיְהִי בֵּיתוֹ בְּדֶרֶךְ מִצְרַיִם. _____

הַדֶּרֶךְ הָיְתָה גְּדוֹלָה וּבֵיתוֹ לֹא גָּדוֹל. _____

_____

הַמַּלְאָךְ יָצָא מִמִּצְרַיִם אֶל בֵּית הַנָּבִיא.

_____

f. הַגּוֹי יָדַע אֶת הָאֱמֶת. _____

וַיֵּדַע כָּל אָדָם אֶת דִּבְרֵי הַבְּרִית. _____

_____

וַיִּתֵּן כָּל אִישׁ צְדָקָה לְאָחִיו. _____

_____

יָד כָּל אִישׁ הָיְתָה בְּיַד אָחִיו. _____

g. וַתִּרְפָּא הָאִשָּׁה אֶת אָבִיהָ וַיֹּאמֶר: רַבָּה גְּבוּרַת הָאֵל! _____

_____ שָׂרָה רִפְּאָה אֶת אָחִיהָ וַתֹּאמֶר: הַלְלוּיָהּ! _____

_____ וַיֹּאמֶר הָאָח אֶל אָבִיו: מִי מוֹשִׁיעֵנוּ? _____

_____ שָׂרָה אָמְרָה: רְפוּאַתְכֶם מִן הַשָּׁמַיִם. _____

Translations

a. Jacob heard/did hear/was hearing the voice of his wife/woman.

Rachel heard/did hear/was hearing the voice/sound of her children.

The man heard/did hear/was hearing/had heard/has heard the sound of the wind.

The woman heard/did hear/was hearing/had heard/has heard the sound of the shofar.

b. You love/do love your wife/woman with all your soul.

Rebekah loved/did love her man/husband with all her heart.

We love/do love our wives/women with all our souls.

Isaac will/may love {Let/may Isaac love} his wife/woman all his life.

c. The family remembered/did remember/was remembering/had remembered/has remembered the blood of the sick ones.

The sick (female) remembered/did remember/was remembering the faces of her family.

Who will/may remember the blood of our sick ones? Who will/may help us?

You help/do help/are helping the sick ones of your family.

d. The servant/slave of the king/sovereign did/was doing/had done/has done mighty deeds/acts.

The servant/slave did/was doing acts/deeds of kindness.

The servant worked/did work/was working from the morning all the day {all day long}.

And in the evening, he did not work/was not working/has not worked/had not worked and [he] did not go out/was not going out/has not gone out/had not gone out of {from} his house.

e. The house of the prophet was/had been between the road and the water.

His house was on the road of {to} Egypt.

The road was/had been big and {but} his house was not/had not been big.

The messenger went out/did go out/was going out/had gone out/has gone out from Egypt to/toward the house of the prophet.

f. The nation/people knew/did know/had known/has known the truth.

All humankind/every person knew/did know the words of the covenant.

Every man gave/did give/was giving *tzedakah* to his brother.

The hand of every man was in the hand of his brother.

g. The woman healed/did heal/was healing her father and he said/did say/was saying, "Great is the might of God!"

Sarah healed/did heal/was healing/had healed/has healed her brother and she said/did say/was saying, "Hallelujah! {Praise *Yah*!}"

The brother said/did say/was saying to his father, "Who is our savior?"

Sarah said/did say/was saying/had said/has said, "Your healing is from the heavens."

Torah Study Text: Genesis 11:1–9

After the well-known narrative of Noah and the ark in Genesis chapters 6–9, and a genealogy of the descendants of Noah in chapter 10, the Torah presents the narrative of the Tower of Babel in Genesis 11:1–9. This is the biblical account of the creation of different languages and the scattering of different peoples across the face of the earth.

Read the Hebrew below to see how many of the words you can recognize. This passage does contain words, Hebrew roots, and grammatical concepts that have not yet been introduced. Underline or circle the words, roots, endings, and prefixes that you already know.

¹וַיְהִי כָל־הָאָרֶץ שָׂפָה אֶחָת וּדְבָרִים אֲחָדִים: ²וַיְהִי בְּנָסְעָם מִקֶּדֶם וַיִּמְצְאוּ בִקְעָה בְּאֶרֶץ שִׁנְעָר וַיֵּשְׁבוּ שָׁם: ³וַיֹּאמְרוּ אִישׁ אֶל־רֵעֵהוּ הָבָה נִלְבְּנָה לְבֵנִים וְנִשְׂרְפָה לִשְׂרֵפָה וַתְּהִי לָהֶם הַלְּבֵנָה לְאָבֶן וְהַחֵמָר הָיָה לָהֶם לַחֹמֶר: ⁴וַיֹּאמְרוּ הָבָה נִבְנֶה־לָּנוּ עִיר וּמִגְדָּל וְרֹאשׁוֹ בַשָּׁמַיִם וְנַעֲשֶׂה־לָּנוּ שֵׁם פֶּן־נָפוּץ עַל־פְּנֵי כָל־הָאָרֶץ: ⁵וַיֵּרֶד יְהֹוָה לִרְאֹת אֶת־הָעִיר וְאֶת־הַמִּגְדָּל אֲשֶׁר בָּנוּ בְּנֵי הָאָדָם: ⁶וַיֹּאמֶר יְהֹוָה הֵן עַם אֶחָד וְשָׂפָה אַחַת לְכֻלָּם וְזֶה הַחִלָּם לַעֲשׂוֹת וְעַתָּה לֹא־יִבָּצֵר מֵהֶם כֹּל אֲשֶׁר יָזְמוּ לַעֲשׂוֹת: ⁷הָבָה נֵרְדָה וְנָבְלָה שָׁם שְׂפָתָם אֲשֶׁר לֹא יִשְׁמְעוּ אִישׁ שְׂפַת רֵעֵהוּ: ⁸וַיָּפֶץ יְהֹוָה אֹתָם מִשָּׁם עַל־פְּנֵי כָל־הָאָרֶץ וַיַּחְדְּלוּ לִבְנֹת הָעִיר: ⁹עַל־כֵּן קָרָא שְׁמָהּ בָּבֶל כִּי־שָׁם בָּלַל יְהֹוָה שְׂפַת כָּל־הָאָרֶץ וּמִשָּׁם הֱפִיצָם יְהֹוָה עַל־פְּנֵי כָל־הָאָרֶץ:

Translating the Torah Study Text

Following is our Torah Study Text, Genesis 11:1–9, reprinted with a literal translation underneath each word. Using your knowledge of the building blocks of the Hebrew language and the meanings of the words provided below, translate this passage into clear English sentences. Write your translation on the lines following the text. This selection includes some grammatical forms and vocabulary that have not yet been introduced. You will need to rely, in part, on the translations provided.

וַיְהִי² וַיְהִי אֲחָדִים וּדְבָרִים אַחַת שָׂפָה הָאָרֶץ כָל־ וַיְהִי¹

| and [it] was | one | and words/ speech | one | language | the earth/ land | all | and [it] was |

שִׁנְעָר בְּאֶרֶץ בִקְעָה וַיִּמְצְאוּ מִקֶּדֶם בְּנָסְעָם

| Shinar | in land | valley/ plain | they found | from east | in/with their journeying/ migrating |

הָבָה רֵעֵהוּ אֶל־ אִישׁ וַיֹּאמְרוּ³ שָׁם: וַיֵּשְׁבוּ

| come | his companion/ neighbor | to | man | and they said | there | and they settled/dwelt |

לְאָבֶן הַלְּבֵנָה לָהֶם וַתְּהִי לִשְׂרֵפָה וְנִשְׂרְפָה לְבֵנִים נִלְבְּנָה

| for stone | the brick | for them | and [it] was | to burning | and let us burn | bricks | let us make |

עִיר לָנוּ נִבְנֶה־ הָבָה וַיֹּאמְרוּ⁴ לַחֹמֶר: לָהֶם הָיָה וְהַחֵמָר

| city | for us | let us build | come | and they said | for mortar | for them | was | and the bitumen |

פֶּן־	שֵׁם	לָּנוּ	וְנַעֲשֶׂה־	בַשָּׁמַיִם	וְרֹאשׁוֹ	וּמִגְדָּל
lest	name	for us	and let us make	in the sky/ heavens	and its top/ head	and tower

לִרְאֹת	יְהוָֹה	וַיֵּרֶד	כָּל־ הָאָרֶץ:	כָּל־	פְּנֵי	עַל־	נָפוּץ
to see	the Eternal	descended/ came down	the earth	all	face of	over	we be scattered/ dispersed

הָאָדָם:	בְּנֵי	בָּנוּ	אֲשֶׁר	הַמִּגְדָּל	וְאֶת־	אֶת־הָעִיר
the man/ humankind	sons/ children of	they built	that	the tower	and	the city

לְכֻלָּם	אַחַת	וְשָׂפָה	אֶחָד	עַם	הֵן	יְהוָֹה	וַיֹּאמֶר
for all of them	one	and language	one	nation/ people	behold/ here/if	the Eternal	said

כֹּל	מֵהֶם	יִבָּצֵר	לֹא־	וְעַתָּה	לַעֲשׂוֹת	הַחִלָּם	וְזֶה
all	from them	be withheld/ inaccessible	not	and now	to do/act	their beginning	and this

וְנָבְלָה	נֵרְדָה	הָבָה	לַעֲשׂוֹת:	יָזְמוּ	אֲשֶׁר
and let us confound	let us go down/descend	come	to do	they may propose/scheme	that

רֵעֵהוּ:	שְׂפַת	אִישׁ	יִשְׁמְעוּ	לֹא	אֲשֶׁר	שְׂפָתָם	שָׁם
his companion/ neighbor	language of	man	they hear/ understand	not	that	their language	there

8 וַיָּ֨פֶץ יְהֹוָ֥ה אֹתָ֛ם מִשָּׁ֖ם עַל־ פְּנֵ֣י כָל־ הָאָ֑רֶץ

| scattered/dispersed | the Eternal | them | from there | over/upon | face of | all | the earth |

וַֽיַּחְדְּל֖וּ לִבְנֹ֥ת הָעִֽיר׃ **9** עַל־כֵּ֞ן קָרָ֤א שְׁמָהּ֙ בָּבֶ֔ל כִּי־

| and they ceased/stopped | to build | the city | therefore | called | its name | Babel | because |

שָׁ֛ם בָּלַ֥ל יְהֹוָ֖ה שְׂפַ֣ת כָּל־ הָאָ֑רֶץ וּמִשָּׁם֙ הֱפִיצָ֣ם

| there | confounded | the Eternal | language of | all | the earth | and from there | scattered them |

יְהֹוָ֔ה עַל־ פְּנֵ֖י כָּל־ הָאָֽרֶץ׃

| the Eternal | over/upon | face of | all | the earth |

TORAH Translations

Compare your translation of Genesis 11:1–9 with the Torah translations below.

¹*Everyone on earth had the same language and the same words. ²And as they migrated from the east, they came upon a valley in the land of Shinar and settled there. ³They said to one another, "Come, let us make bricks and burn them hard."—Brick served them as stone, and bitumen served them as mortar.—⁴And they said, "Come, let us build us a city, and a tower with its top in the sky, to make a name for ourselves; else we shall be scattered all over the world." ⁵The LORD came down to look at the city and tower that man had built, ⁶and the LORD said, "If, as one people with one language for all, this is how they have begun to act, then nothing that they may propose to do will be out of their reach. ⁷Let us, then, go down and confound their speech there, so that they shall not understand one another's speech." ⁸Thus the LORD scattered them from there over the face of the whole earth; and they stopped building the city. ⁹That is why it was called Babel, because there the LORD confounded the*

speech of the whole earth; and from there the Lord *scattered them over the face of the whole earth.*

JPS Hebrew-English Tanakh: The Traditional Hebrew Text and the New JPS Translation—2d Ed. Philadelphia: The Jewish Publication Society, 1999.

¹The whole earth was of one language and of common purpose. ²And it came to pass, when they migrated from the east they found a plain in the land of Shinar and settled there. ³They said to one another, "Come, let us make bricks and burn them in fire." And the brick served them as stone, and the lime served them as mortar. ⁴And they said, "Come, let us build us a city, and a tower with its top in the heavens, and let us make a name for ourselves, lest we be dispersed across the whole earth."

*⁵*Hashem *descended to look at the city and tower which the sons of man built, ⁶and* Hashem *said, "Behold, they are one people with one language for all, and this they begin to do! And now, should it not be withheld from them all they propose to do? ⁷Come, let us descend and there confuse their language, that they should not understand one another's language."*

⁸And Hashem *dispersed them from there over the face of the whole earth; and they stopped building the city. ⁹That is why it was called Babel, because it was there that* Hashem *confused the language of the whole earth, and from there* Hashem *scattered them over the face of the whole earth.*

The Chumash, ArtScroll Series, Stone Edition. Brooklyn: Mesorah Publications, 1993.

¹Now all the earth was of one language and one set-of-words.

²And it was when they migrated to the east that they found a valley in the land of Shinar and settled there.

³They said, each man to his neighbor:

Come-now! Let us bake bricks and let us burn them well-burnt!

So for them brick-stone was like building-stone, and raw-bitumen was for them like red-mortar.

⁴Now they said:

Come-now! Let us build ourselves a city and a tower, its top in the heavens,

and let us make ourselves a name,

lest we be scattered over the face of all the earth!

⁵But Yhwh *came down to look over the city and the tower that the humans were building.*

*⁶*Yhwh *said:*

Here, (they are) one people with one language for them all, and this is merely the first

CHAPTER 5

52

of their doings—

now there will be no barrier for them in all that they scheme to do!

⁷Come-now! Let us go down and there let us baffle their language,

so that no man will understand the language of his neighbor.

*⁸So Y*HWH *scattered them from there over the face of all the earth, and they had to stop building the city.*

*⁹Therefore its name was called Bavel/Babble, for there Y*HWH *baffled the language of all the earth-folk, and from there, Y*HWH *scattered them over the face of all the earth.*

THE FIVE BOOKS OF MOSES: A NEW TRANSLATION WITH INTRODUCTIONS, COMMENTARY, AND NOTES BY EVERETT FOX. NEW YORK: SCHOCKEN BOOKS, 1995.

*And the whole earth was of one language, and of one speech. And it came to pass, as they journeyed from the east, that they found a plain in the land of Shin'ar; and they dwelt there. And they said to one another, Come, let us make bricks, and burn them thoroughly. And they had brick for stone, and slime had they for mortar. And they said, Come, let us build us a city and a tower, whose top may reach to heaven; and let us make us a name, lest we be scattered abroad upon the face of the whole earth. And the L*ORD *came down to see the city and the tower, which the children of men were building. And the L*ORD *said, Behold, the people is one, and they have all one language; and this they begin to do: and now nothing will be withheld from them, which they have schemed to do. Come, let us go down, and there confound their language, that they may not understand one another's speech. So the L*ORD *scattered them abroad from there upon the face of all the earth: and they ceased to build the city. Therefore is the name of it called Bavel; because the L*ORD *did there confound the language of all the earth: and from thence did the L*ORD *scatter them abroad upon the face of all the earth.*

THE JERUSALEM BIBLE, PUBLISHED FOR THE NAHUM ZEEV WILLIAMS FAMILY FOUNDATION AT HECHAL SHLOMO, JERUSALEM. JERUSALEM: KOREN PUBLISHERS JERUSALEM LTD., 1969.

Vocabulary

Locate each of the following words in the Torah Study Text: Genesis 11:1–9.

one *m*	—	אֶחָד
one *f*	—	אַחַת
friend, companion, fellow, neighbor *m*	—	רֵעַ
stone *f*	—	אֶבֶן
city *f*	—	עִיר
head, top, beginning *m*	—	רֹאשׁ
there	—	שָׁם

Notes on the Vocabulary

1. In Hebrew, the word "one" acts as an adjective, with four forms:

   f pl אֲחָדוֹת   *m pl* אֲחָדִים   *f sg* אַחַת   *m sg* אֶחָד

   The plural forms can sometimes be translated as "a few" or "some."

2. The word רֵעַ has a range of meanings. The idiom אִישׁ...רֵעֵהוּ, which appears in our Torah Study Text in verses 3 and 7, can be translated as "one...another."

The basic meaning of the root יָ־שָׁ־ב is "sit," "settle," or "dwell." This root follows the ◼◽וֹ◼ participle pattern. The following are the four participle forms:

   f pl יוֹשְׁבוֹת   *m pl* יוֹשְׁבִים   *f sg* יוֹשֶׁבֶת   *m sg* יוֹשֵׁב

The perfect and imperfect forms can be found in the verb charts in the back of the book. The root יָ־שָׁ־ב appears only once in this chapter's Torah Study Text:

(verse 2)

and they settled/dwelt there	—	וַיֵּשְׁבוּ שָׁם

The following words, both ancient and modern, are derived from the root יָ־שָׁ־ב. The first root letter יֹ drops out in some words formed from this root.

chairperson	—	יוֹשֵׁב רֹאשׁ

population, settlement	—	יִשּׁוּב
sedentary	—	יְשִׁיב
sitting, residence, session, yeshivah *(Jewish religious academy)*	—	יְשִׁיבָה
colonization	—	יִשְׁבָנוּת
seat, abode, residence, moshav *(cooperative settlement)*	—	מוֹשָׁב
settler	—	מִתְיַשֵּׁב
resident, inhabitant, sojourner	—	תּוֹשָׁב
seat, dwelling	—	שֶׁבֶת
base, pedestal, chassis *(of a vehicle)*	—	תּוֹשֶׁבֶת

The basic meaning of the root בּ־נ־ה is "build." This root follows the ▢▢וֹ participle pattern. It is slightly irregular, because the final root letter is ה, which disappears in some verb forms. The following are the four participle forms:

f pl בּוֹנוֹת   *m pl* בּוֹנִים   *f sg* בּוֹנָה   *m sg* בּוֹנֶה

The perfect and imperfect forms can be found in the verb charts in the back of the book.

The root בּ־נ־ה appears three times in our Torah Study Text, in verses 4, 5, and 8:

(verse 4)

Come, let us build for us a city	—	הָבָה נִבְנֶה־לָּנוּ עִיר

(verse 5)

that the children of humankind had built	—	אֲשֶׁר בָּנוּ בְּנֵי הָאָדָם

(verse 8)

they ceased to build the city	—	וַיַּחְדְּלוּ לִבְנֹת הָעִיר

The following words, both ancient and modern, are derived from the root בּ־נ־ה. The last root letter ה drops out in some words formed from this root.

structure, building	—	בִּנְיָן
built-up	—	בָּנוּי
construction	—	בְּנִיָּה
structure, formation, format	—	מִבְנֶה
structural	—	מִבְנִי
Yavneh (*ancient city—Jewish center after the fall of Jerusalem*)	—	יַבְנֶה
model, pattern, image	—	תַבְנִית

Torah Commentary

In verse 5, those who are building the tower are called בְּנֵי הָאָדָם, "the children of Adam/humankind," instead of merely "the people" or "the builders." Rashi cites a midrash (*B'reishit Rabbah* 38:9) that suggests this wording implies a spiritual connection between the builders of the Tower of Babel and the original Adam, both having demonstrated a lack of gratitude to God.

בְּנֵי הָאָדָם, **the children of Adam/humankind.** *Who else's children could they be? The children of donkeys or camels? [Why bother stating that they are children of Adam/humankind?] Rather, [this teaches that they are] the children of the first Adam, who was ungrateful and said [in Genesis 3:12]: "The woman whom You gave to be with me...[she gave me from the tree and I ate"—implying that God is to blame for giving Adam that woman]. So, these people too were ungrateful, in rebelling against the One who had bestowed blessing upon them and saved them from the Flood [in the time of Noah].*

RASHI ON GENESIS 11:5

The following Chasidic commentary expands upon the above Rashi, adding a positive twist at the end.

What does the Torah mean when it says בְּנֵי הָאָדָם "the children of men"? Who else could they be? donkeys? camels? Rather, this refers to the children of Adam, the first man, who was ungrateful to God after He had given him Eve, and said, "the woman which You gave me" (Gen. 3:12). Here too they were ungrateful and rebelled against God, after He had saved them from the Flood (Rashi). The attributes, characteristics, and influences of the impulses embedded within a person carry over for a number of genera- tions after him. This embedded attribute of ungratefulness, which had been revealed in

Adam, continued in mankind through to the generation of the Tower of Babel, and these were indeed "the children of Adam," children of the same Adam who showed his ingratitude. From this we can see how when a person improves his attributes by working at them, the effect of his actions will be felt for generations to come.

R. Zvi Natan Finkel, the elder of Slobodka, as quoted in *Torah Gems*, comp. Aharon Yaakov Greenberg, trans. R. Dr. Shmuel Himelstein. Tel Aviv and Brooklyn: Yavneh Publishing House, Chemed Books, 1998.

Both verses 8 and 9, using slightly different wording, state that God scattered the people. Since the same thing does not need to be stated twice, Rashi cites a talmudic reference (BT *Sanhedrin* 107b), which applies a different meaning to each of these verses. Rashi then goes on to reflect upon the difference in punishment received by the generation of the Flood (at the time of Noah) and that of the Tower of Babel, citing a midrash from *B'reishit Rabbah* 38:6.

וַיָּפֶץ יְהוָֹה אֹתָם מִשָּׁם *(verse 8), **The Eternal scattered/dispersed them from there.*** *In this world. What they had said [in verse 4]:* פֶּן נָפוּץ, *"lest we be scattered/dispersed," really happened to them.*

וּמִשָּׁם הֱפִיצָם *(verse 9), **and from there [the Eternal] scattered them.*** *This teaches that they have no share in the world to come (BT* Sanhedrin *107b).*

Which act was worse, that of the generation of the Flood or that of the generation of the dispersion? The former did not stretch out their hand against God, and the latter did stretch out their hand against God to war against Him. Yet the former were drowned, and the latter did not perish from the world! This is because the generation of the Flood were robbers and there was strife among them; therefore, they were destroyed. The latter behaved with love and friendship among them, as it is said [in verse 1]: שָׂפָה אֶחָת וּדְבָרִים אֲחָדִים, ***"[they had] one language and one words."*** *You learn [from this] that strife is hateful [to God] and great is peace.*

RASHI ON GENESIS 11:8–9

Exercises

1. Make flash cards for each of the new vocabulary words and Hebrew roots introduced in this chapter, or use the flash card set published as a companion to this book. Review the cards to learn all of them.

2. Draw a line connecting each Hebrew word to its English translation. For some words, there can be more than one correct translation.

friend	אֶבֶן
stone	שָׁם
there	רֵעַ
fellow	
head	אַחַת
one	
beginning	רֹאשׁ
companion	
city	אֶחָד
top	
neighbor	עִיר

3. The following are singular and plural forms of words introduced as vocabulary in this chapter. Draw a line connecting each plural word to its singular form. Translate both into English.

	plural	singular	
_____	עָרִים	רֵעַ	_____
_____	רָאשִׁים	אֶבֶן	_____
_____	אֲחָדִים	אַחַת	_____
_____	אֲבָנִים	עִיר	_____
_____	אֲחָדוֹת	רֹאשׁ	_____
_____	רֵעִים	אֶחָד	_____

4. Read and translate the following groups of words.

b. רֵעַ טוֹב _____

אָח וָרֵעַ _____

אֵשֶׁת רֵעֵהוּ _____

דַּם רֵעֶךָ _____

פְּנֵי רֵעֶךָ _____

a. אִישׁ אֶחָד _____

אִשָּׁה אַחַת _____

רוּחַ אֶחָד _____

יוֹם אֶחָד _____

יָמִים אֲחָדִים _____

d. רֹאשׁ הָאֲנָשִׁים _____

רֹאשׁ בְּנֵי יִשְׂרָאֵל _____

רֹאשׁ הַגּוֹיִים _____

רֹאשׁ רֵעֵהוּ _____

רָאשֵׁי הַגִּבּוֹרִים _____

c. אֶבֶן גְּדוֹלָה _____

אֲבָנִים גְּדוֹלוֹת _____

אֲבָנִים אֲחָדוֹת _____

לֵב אֶבֶן _____

אַבְנֵי יְרוּשָׁלַיִם _____

f. שֵׁם _____

שֵׁם הַנָּשִׁים _____

הַמַּיִם אֲשֶׁר שָׁם _____

מִשָּׁם _____

הָאוֹר מִשָּׁם _____

e. עִיר הַנָּבִיא _____

עִיר הַצַּדִּיק _____

עִיר הַקֹּדֶשׁ _____

עוֹבְדֵי הָעִיר _____

יוֹשְׁבֵי הֶעָרִים _____

5. Identify the root of each of the following participles, and whether the participle form is masculine or feminine, singular or plural. Translate the meaning of the root.

m/f	sing/pl	Translation	Root	Participle
_____	_____	_____	_____	בּוֹנִים
_____	_____	_____	_____	עוֹשִׂים
_____	_____	_____	_____	עוֹבֵד
_____	_____	_____	_____	יוֹשְׁבִים
_____	_____	_____	_____	מְחַיֶּה

אוֹהֶבֶת
יוֹשֵׁב
זוֹכְרוֹת
אוֹמְרִים
יוֹצֵא
בּוֹנֶה
יוֹדֵעַ

Rashi

The Torah commentaries cited in this chapter are from Rabbi Shlomo ben Isaac, a medieval scholar who wrote commentaries on both the Torah and the Talmud. Rabbi Shlomo ben Isaac lived from 1040 to 1105, spending most of his life in Troyes, France. He is most commonly known as Rashi, רַשִׁי, an acronym formed from the first letters of his name:

רַב שְׁלֹמֹה בֶּן יִצְחָק

Rashi's commentaries continue to be widely studied today and are very useful aids to students of Torah and Talmud. Much of his commentary comes from prior rabbinic sources, which Rashi compiled and made accessible to the student. His aim was to provide a clear explanation of the simple meaning of the text, elucidating difficult words or phrases, and providing midrashic interpretations where they served to clarify textual difficulties.

In most texts, Rashi's commentary appears without vowels in a distinctive lettering style known as "Rashi script." "Rashi script" was never actually used by Rashi himself; it was created after the advent of the printing press to make a visible distinction between the appearance of the commentary and the actual biblical or talmudic text. Below are the first words of this chapter's Torah Study Text, Genesis 11:1, as it appears in our regular print and as it would appear in Rashi script:

וַיְהִי כָל־הָאָרֶץ שָׂפָה אֶחָת
ויהי כל־האָרץ שפה אחת

The following is the Hebrew alphabet in our regular print and in Rashi script:

א ב ג ד ה ו ז ח ט י כ ל מ נ ס ע פ צ ק ר ש ת
א ב ג ד ה ו ז ח ט י כ ל מ נ ס ע פ צ ק ר ש ת

Torah Study Text: Vocabulary and Root Review

This unit's Torah Study Text, Genesis 11:1–9, is reprinted below, highlighting the new vocabulary words as well as the words formed from the new Hebrew roots introduced in Chapter 5. Read this passage again, recalling the meaning of each of the highlighted words or roots.

¹וַיְהִי כָל־הָאָרֶץ שָׂפָה **אֶחָת** וּדְבָרִים **אֲחָדִים**: ²וַיְהִי בְּנָסְעָם מִקֶּדֶם וַיִּמְצְאוּ בִקְעָה בְּאֶרֶץ שִׁנְעָר וַיֵּשְׁבוּ **שָׁם**: ³וַיֹּאמְרוּ אִישׁ אֶל־**רֵעֵהוּ** הָבָה נִלְבְּנָה לְבֵנִים וְנִשְׂרְפָה לִשְׂרֵפָה וַתְּהִי לָהֶם הַלְּבֵנָה לְ**אָבֶן** וְהַחֵמָר הָיָה לָהֶם לַחֹמֶר: ⁴וַיֹּאמְרוּ הָבָה **נִבְנֶה**־לָּנוּ **עִיר** וּמִגְדָּל **וְרֹאשׁוֹ** בַשָּׁמַיִם וְנַעֲשֶׂה־לָּנוּ שֵׁם פֶּן־נָפוּץ עַל־פְּנֵי כָל־הָאָרֶץ: ⁵וַיֵּרֶד יְהוָה לִרְאֹת אֶת־הָ**עִיר** וְאֶת־הַמִּגְדָּל אֲשֶׁר **בָּנוּ** בְּנֵי הָאָדָם: ⁶וַיֹּאמֶר יְהוָה הֵן עַם **אֶחָד** וְשָׂפָה **אַחַת** לְכֻלָּם וְזֶה הַחִלָּם לַעֲשׂוֹת וְעַתָּה לֹא־יִבָּצֵר מֵהֶם כֹּל אֲשֶׁר יָזְמוּ לַעֲשׂוֹת: ⁷הָבָה נֵרְדָה וְנָבְלָה **שָׁם** שְׂפָתָם אֲשֶׁר לֹא יִשְׁמְעוּ אִישׁ שְׂפַת **רֵעֵהוּ**: ⁸וַיָּפֶץ יְהוָה אֹתָם מִ**שָּׁם** עַל־פְּנֵי כָל־הָאָרֶץ וַיַּחְדְּלוּ לִ**בְנֹת** הָעִיר: ⁹עַל־כֵּן קָרָא שְׁמָהּ בָּבֶל כִּי־**שָׁם** בָּלַל יְהוָה שְׂפַת כָּל־הָאָרֶץ וּמִ**שָּׁם** הֱפִיצָם יְהוָה עַל־פְּנֵי כָל־הָאָרֶץ:

Building Blocks

Plural Verb Forms

As stated earlier, there are many different verb patterns in Hebrew. In Chapters 2 and 4, we introduced masculine and feminine forms of the simplest Hebrew verb pattern. The forms introduced were all singular. In this chapter, we introduce the corresponding plural verb forms.

Plural Perfect Verbs

The plural perfect form, used for both masculine and feminine subjects, is as follows:

‫וּ◼◼ ◼ָ‬

Examples:

[he] said	—	אָמַר	[he] sat	—	יָשַׁב
[she] said	—	אָמְרָה	[she] sat	—	יָשְׁבָה
[they] said	—	אָמְרוּ	[they] sat	—	יָשְׁבוּ

Remember that verbs can be translated in more than one way. The root י־שׁ־ב can mean "sit," "settle," or "dwell." Perfect verbs describe completed action, which can be expressed in various ways in English.

Plural Imperfect Verbs

For imperfect verbs, there are separate masculine and feminine plural forms. The masculine plural form is as follows:

‫וּ◼◼ ◼ְ י‬

This form is used with mixed-gender groups as well as all-masculine groups. The feminine plural imperfect form, used only for all-feminine groups, is . It is mentioned here for enrichment only. It is not necessary to memorize this form, as it appears very infrequently in the Bible and virtually never in the prayer book. It will not be used in the exercises in this book.

Examples:

[he] will/may say	—	יֹאמַר	[he] will/may work	—	יַעֲבֹד
[she] will/may say	—	תֹּאמַר	[she] will/may work	—	תַּעֲבֹד
[they] will/may say	—	יֹאמְרוּ	[they] will/may work	—	יַעֲבְדוּ

Remember that imperfect verbs can indicate the future tense, ongoing incompleted action, or action that is wished or urged. The examples above could be translated in various different ways.

The Endings םָ and הֶם

In *Aleph Isn't Enough*, we introduced several pronoun endings, such as ךְ, meaning "your" or "you," and נוּ, meaning "our" or "us." Similarly, the endings םָ and הֶם mean "their" or "them." They refer to all-masculine groups or mixed-gender groups.

When attached to a preposition, these endings mean "them." Examples:

in them, with them	—	בָּם	in, with —	בְּ
to them, for them	—	לָהֶם	to, for —	לְ
to them, toward them	—	אֲלֵיהֶם	to, toward —	אֶל

The ending םָ also means "them" when attached to a verb. The following example is from Deuteronomy 6:9 (the *V'ahavta*):

[and] write	—	וְכָתַבְתָּ
[and] write them on the doorposts of your house	—	וּכְתַבְתָּם עַל־מְזוּזֹת בֵּיתֶךָ

When attached to a noun, the םָ and הֶם endings mean "their." The םָ ending is used with singular nouns, and the הֶם ending is used with plural nouns. Examples:

their blood	—	דָּמָם	blood —	דָּם
their face, their faces	—	פְּנֵיהֶם	face, faces —	פָּנִים
their voices	—	קוֹלוֹתֵיהֶם	voices —	קוֹלוֹת

Torah Study Text with Building Blocks

Following is this unit's Torah Study Text, Genesis 11:1–9, reprinted with the new Building Blocks highlighted. Reread these verses, noting the appearance of plural perfect and imperfect verbs, with and without the reversing *vav*, and the use of the םָ and הֶם endings. A translation is provided below for only the highlighted Building Blocks. Remember that there could be other possible translations. For a full translation of the verses, refer back to Chapter 5.

¹וַיְהִי כָל־הָאָרֶץ שָׂפָה אֶחָת וּדְבָרִים אֲחָדִים: ²וַיְהִי בְּנָסְעָ**ם** מִקֶּדֶם **וַיִּמְצְאוּ** בִקְעָה בְּאֶרֶץ שִׁנְעָר **וַיֵּשְׁבוּ** שָׁם: ³**וַיֹּאמְרוּ** אִישׁ אֶל־רֵעֵהוּ הָבָה נִלְבְּנָה לְבֵנִים וְנִשְׂרְפָה לִשְׂרֵפָה וַתְּהִי לָ**הֶם** הַלְּבֵנָה לְאָבֶן וְהַחֵמָר הָיָה לָ**הֶם** לַחֹמֶר: ⁴**וַיֹּאמְרוּ** הָבָה נִבְנֶה־לָּנוּ עִיר וּמִגְדָּל וְרֹאשׁוֹ בַשָּׁמַיִם וְנַעֲשֶׂה־לָּנוּ שֵׁם פֶּן־נָפוּץ עַל־פְּנֵי כָל־הָאָרֶץ: ⁵וַיֵּרֶד יְהוָה לִרְאֹת אֶת־הָעִיר וְאֶת־הַמִּגְדָּל אֲשֶׁר **בָּנוּ** בְּנֵי הָאָדָם: ⁶וַיֹּאמֶר יְהוָה הֵן עַם אֶחָד וְשָׂפָה אַחַת לְכֻלָּ**ם** וְזֶה הַחִלָּם לַעֲשׂוֹת וְעַתָּה לֹא־יִבָּצֵר מֵהֶם כֹּל אֲשֶׁר **יָזְמוּ** לַעֲשׂוֹת: ⁷הָבָה נֵרְדָה וְנָבְלָה שָׁם שְׂפָתָ**ם** אֲשֶׁר לֹא **יִשְׁמְעוּ** אִישׁ שְׂפַת רֵעֵהוּ: ⁸וַיָּפֶץ יְהוָה אֹתָ**ם** מִשָּׁם עַל־פְּנֵי כָל־הָאָרֶץ **וַיַּחְדְּלוּ** לִבְנֹת הָעִיר: ⁹עַל־כֵּן קָרָא שְׁמָהּ בָּבֶל כִּי־שָׁם בָּלַל יְהוָה שְׂפַת כָּל־הָאָרֶץ וּמִשָּׁם הֱפִיצָ**ם** יְהוָה עַל־פְּנֵי כָל־הָאָרֶץ:

in/with their migrating/journeying	—	בְּנָסְעָ**ם**
[and] they found	—	וַיִּמְצְאוּ
[and] they settled/dwelt	—	וַיֵּשְׁבוּ
[and] they said	—	וַיֹּאמְרוּ
to/for them	—	לָ**הֶם**
they built	—	בָּנוּ
all of them (כָּל with ם◌ַ ending)	—	לְכֻלָּ**ם**
they may propose/scheme	—	יָזְמוּ
their language	—	שְׂפָתָ**ם**
they hear/understand	—	יִשְׁמְעוּ
them (אֶת with ם◌ַ ending)	—	אֹתָ**ם**
[and] they ceased/stopped	—	וַיַּחְדְּלוּ
scattered them	—	הֱפִיצָ**ם**

Plural Forms

Enrichment (GRAMMAR)

The following chart includes the participle, perfect, and imperfect masculine plural forms for every root introduced thus far that follows the simple pattern. Remember that all the perfect forms are also feminine forms, and the imperfect forms are used with mixed-gender as well as all-masculine groups. This chart present the regular vowels for each form, but alternate or irregular vowels sometimes appear in biblical texts. Keep in mind that this chart is included for enrichment only. It is not necessary to memorize these forms.

It may be helpful to notice certain variations:

• In roots that end with the letter ה, such as ב־נ־ה, ה־י־ה, and ע־שׂ־ה, the root letter ה drops out in all the plural forms.

• In many roots that begin with the letter י or the letter נ, such as י־שׁ־ב, י־צ־א, י־ד־ע, and נ־ת־ן, that first root letter י or נ drops out in the imperfect forms.

	Imperfect	Perfect	Participle	Root	
	יֶאֱהָבוּ	אָהֲבוּ	אוֹהֲבִים	א־ה־ב	love
	יֹאכְלוּ	אָכְלוּ	אוֹכְלִים	א־כ־ל	eat
	יֹאמְרוּ	אָמְרוּ	אוֹמְרִים	א־מ־ר	say
	יִבְחֲרוּ	בָּחֲרוּ	בּוֹחֲרִים	ב־ח־ר	choose
(final ה drops out)	יִבְנוּ	בָּנוּ	בּוֹנִים	ב־נ־ה	build
(final ה drops out)	יִהְיוּ	הָיוּ	–	ה־י־ה	be
	יִזְכְּרוּ	זָכְרוּ	זוֹכְרִים	ז־כ־ר	remember
(irregular imperfect— root letter י missing)	יֵדְעוּ	יָדְעוּ	יוֹדְעִים	י־ד־ע	know
	יֵצְאוּ	יָצְאוּ	יוֹצְאִים	י־צ־א	go out
	יֵשְׁבוּ	יָשְׁבוּ	יוֹשְׁבִים	י־שׁ־ב	sit, dwell
	יִמְלְכוּ	מָלְכוּ	מוֹלְכִים	מ־ל־ך	rule
(irregular imperfect— root letter נ missing)	יִתְּנוּ	נָתְנוּ	נוֹתְנִים	נ־ת־ן	give
	יַעַבְדוּ	עָבְדוּ	עוֹבְדִים	ע־ב־ד	work, serve
	יַעַזְרוּ	עָזְרוּ	עוֹזְרִים	ע־ז־ר	help
(final ה drops out)	יַעֲשׂוּ	עָשׂוּ	עוֹשִׂים	ע־שׂ־ה	make, do
	יִרְפְּאוּ	רָפְאוּ	רוֹפְאִים	ר־פ־א	heal
	יִשְׁמְעוּ	שָׁמְעוּ	שׁוֹמְעִים	שׁ־מ־ע	hear
	יִשְׁמְרוּ	שָׁמְרוּ	שׁוֹמְרִים	שׁ־מ־ר	guard, keep

CHAPTER 6

Additional Reading and Translation Practice

Translate the following excerpts from the Bible and the prayer book, using the extra vocabulary words provided. Check your translations against the English translations that follow.

1. From וְשָׁמְרוּ (Exodus 31:16)—This song comes from a biblical passage regarding the observance of Shabbat and is included in Shabbat evening and morning services. This is the first line of the song, and it begins with a plural perfect verb with a reversing *vav*.

to make (*from the root* עׂ-שׁ-ה) — לַעֲשׂוֹת

generations — דוֹרוֹת

וְשָׁמְרוּ בְנֵי־יִשְׂרָאֵל אֶת־הַשַּׁבָּת, לַעֲשׂוֹת אֶת־הַשַּׁבָּת לְדֹרֹתָם
בְּרִית עוֹלָם:

_____

_____

2. From אַשְׁרֵי (Psalm 84:5)—This verse is included in the introductory section of the morning and afternoon service. The entire text of אַשְׁרֵי consists of this verse (Psalm 84:5), followed by Psalm 144:15, the entire text of Psalm 145, and Psalm 115:18. The new root יָ-שׁ-ב appears as a participle in a word pair. The root הָ-לֵ-ל appears as a plural imperfect verb with the ending וּ attached.

happy, fortunate — אַשְׁרֵי

still, yet, more — עוֹד

selah *(concluding word in certain psalms and in liturgy)* — סֶלָה

אַשְׁרֵי יוֹשְׁבֵי בֵיתֶךָ, עוֹד יְהַלְלוּךָ סֶּלָה:

_____

3. From בִּרְכַּת הַמָּזוֹן—The Blessing after Meals has several parts, including the following blessing for Jerusalem. The new root בָּ-נָ-ה appears twice in this excerpt, as a command form and as a participle.

build (*command form from the root* בָּ-נָ-ה) — בְּנֵה

soon, quickly — בִּמְהֵרָה

וּבְנֵה יְרוּשָׁלַיִם עִיר הַקֹּדֶשׁ בִּמְהֵרָה בְיָמֵינוּ. בָּרוּךְ אַתָּה יְיָ,
בּוֹנֶה בְרַחֲמָיו יְרוּשָׁלָיִם. אָמֵן.

_____

_____

4. Psalm 118:1–4—This passage is included in *Hallel* (Psalms 113–118), the collection of psalms in praise of God recited on festivals. The root אָ־מַ־ר appears in both singular and plural imperfect forms.

give thanks	—	הוֹדוּ
because, that	—	כִּי
let (*a term of entreaty, sometimes* *translated as* please)	—	נָא
Aaron	—	אַהֲרֹן
reverers of, those who revere	—	יִרְאֵי

¹הוֹדוּ לַיהוָה כִּי־טוֹב כִּי לְעוֹלָם חַסְדּוֹ: ²יֹאמַר־נָא יִשְׂרָאֵל כִּי
לְעוֹלָם חַסְדּוֹ: ³יֹאמְרוּ־נָא בֵית־אַהֲרֹן כִּי לְעוֹלָם חַסְדּוֹ: ⁴יֹאמְרוּ־נָא
יִרְאֵי יְהוָה כִּי לְעוֹלָם חַסְדּוֹ:

_____

_____

_____

5. From יִשְׂמְחוּ—This song is the part of the Shabbat liturgy. Three plural imperfect verbs appear in this excerpt.

plural imperfect verb from the root שָׂ־מַ־ח, rejoice	—	יִשְׂמְחוּ
kingdom, dominion	—	מַלְכוּת
proclaimers of, those who proclaim	—	קוֹרְאֵי
pleasure, delight	—	עֹנֶג
seventh	—	שְׁבִיעִי
all of them (כֹּל) *with the ending*		

□ָ *attached*)	—	כֻּלָּם
plural imperfect verb from the *root* שׂ־בׄ־ע, **be satiated, content** —		יִשְׂבְּעוּ
plural imperfect verb from the *root* ע־נ־ג, **have pleasure, delight** —		וְיִתְעַנְּגוּ

יִשְׂמְחוּ בְמַלְכוּתְךָ שׁוֹמְרֵי שַׁבָּת וְקוֹרְאֵי עֹנֶג, עַם מְקַדְּשֵׁי שְׁבִיעִי, כֻּלָּם יִשְׂבְּעוּ וְיִתְעַנְּגוּ מִטּוּבֶךָ.

_____

_____

6. From Isaiah 2:2–4—This passage is a prophetic vision of a future time of peace and well-being. A portion of verse 2:3 appears in the Torah service, and the end of verse 2:4 has become a well-known folk song. In verse 2:2, the root ה־י־ה appears as both a perfect verb with a reversing *vav* and an imperfect verb.

From Isaiah 2:2

end	—	אַחֲרִית
firm, established	—	נָכוֹן
mountain	—	הַר
plural perfect verb with reversing vav *from the* *root* נ־ה־ר, **flow, stream** —		וְנָהֲרוּ

²וְהָיָה בְּאַחֲרִית הַיָּמִים נָכוֹן יִהְיֶה הַר בֵּית־יְהוָֹה בְּרֹאשׁ הֶהָרִים... וְנָהֲרוּ אֵלָיו כָּל־הַגּוֹיִם:

_____

_____

From Isaiah 2:3

plural perfect verb with reversing vav *from the root* ה־ל־ך, **go** —		וְהָלְכוּ
let us go up	—	לְכוּ וְנַעֲלֶה
mountain	—	הַר

for, because	—	כִּי
feminine imperfect verb from the *root* י־צ־א, go out, go forth	—	תֵּצֵא

³וְהָלְכוּ עַמִּים רַבִּים וְאָמְרוּ לְכוּ וְנַעֲלֶה אֶל־הַר־יְהוָֹה אֶל־בֵּית
אֱלֹהֵי יַעֲקֹב...כִּי מִצִּיּוֹן תֵּצֵא תוֹרָה וּדְבַר־יְהוָֹה מִירוּשָׁלָ͏ִם:

_____

_____

_____

From Isaiah 2:4

perfect verb with reversing vav *from the* *root* שׁ־פ־ט, judge	—	וְשָׁפַט
plural perfect verb with reversing vav *from the root* כ־ת־ת, beat	—	וְכִתְּתוּ
sword	—	חֶרֶב
plowshares	—	אִתִּים
spear	—	חֲנִית
pruning knives	—	מַזְמֵרוֹת
imperfect verb from the root נ־שׂ־א, raise, lift up	—	יִשָּׂא
plural imperfect verb from the root ל־מ־ד, study, learn	—	יִלְמְדוּ
still, [any] more	—	עוֹד
war	—	מִלְחָמָה

וְשָׁפַט בֵּין הַגּוֹיִם...וְכִתְּתוּ חַרְבוֹתָם לְאִתִּים וַחֲנִיתוֹתֵיהֶם
לְמַזְמֵרוֹת לֹא־יִשָּׂא גוֹי אֶל־גּוֹי חֶרֶב וְלֹא־יִלְמְדוּ עוֹד מִלְחָמָה:

_____

_____

_____

Translations

1. From וְשָׁמְרוּ (Exodus 31:16)—The Children of Israel/Israelites will keep {let/may the children of Israel keep} the Sabbath, to make the Sabbath for their generations a covenant of eternity {an eternal covenant}.

2. From אַשְׁרֵי (Psalm 84:5)—Happy/fortunate are the sitters/dwellers of Your house {those who sit/dwell in Your house}, they will/may they/let them still/yet/more praise You. Selah.

3. From בִּרְכַּת הַמָּזוֹן—And build Jerusalem, the city of holiness {the Holy City}, soon in our days. Blessed are you, Eternal One, {the One who} builds in God's {His} compassion/mercy Jerusalem. Amen.

4. Psalm 118:1–4—Give thanks to the Eternal One because [He/It is] good, because forever is God's {His} kindness. Let Israel say that forever is God's {His} kindness. Let the house of Aaron say that forever is God's {His} kindness. Let those who revere the Eternal One say that forever is God's {His} kindness.

5. From יִשְׂמְחוּ—They will/may they/let them rejoice in Your dominion the keepers/ guardians of Shabbat and those who proclaim [it] a pleasure/delight. {Let/may those who keep the Sabbath and proclaim it a delight rejoice in Your dominion.} A people/nation, sanctifiers of [the] seventh [day], all of them will/may/let them be satiated/content and have pleasure/delight from Your goodness.

6. From Isaiah 2:2—And it will be in the end of days, firm/established will be the mountain of the House of the Eternal at the top of the mountains {the mountain of the House of the Eternal will be firm/established at the top of the mountains}...and they will stream/flow to it all the nations/peoples {and all the nations/peoples will stream/flow to it}.

   From Isaiah 2:3—And they will go many nations/peoples {And many nations/peoples will go} and they will say, "Let us go up to the mountain of the Eternal One, to the House of the God of Jacob...for from Zion will go forth Torah {let/may Torah go forth} and the word of the Eternal from Jerusalem."

   From Isaiah 2:4—And God {He} will judge among the nations/peoples...and they will beat their swords to plowshares and their spears to pruning knives. Nation/people will not lift up sword toward {against} nation/people, and they will not still/{any}more study/learn war.

Exercises

1. Read and translate the following groups of words.

.b	יָדְךָ	.a	רֹאשׁוֹ
	יָדָם		רֹאשָׁהּ
	יְדֵיהֶם		רֹאשְׁךָ
	יָדוֹ		רֹאשָׁם
	יָדָהּ		רָאשֵׁיהֶם
	יָדֶיהָ		רָאשֵׁיכֶם

.d	רוּחוֹ	.c	פָּנֶיךָ
	רוּחָהּ		פָּנֶיהָ
	רוּחֵנוּ		פְּנֵיכֶם
	רוּחוֹתֵינוּ		פָּנָיו
	רוּחָם		פְּנֵיהֶם
	רוּחוֹתֵיהֶם		פָּנֵינוּ

.f	לְבָבְךָ	.e	רֵעֲךָ
	לִבְּךָ		רֵעֵהוּ
	לְבָבָם		רֵעָיו
	לִבָּם		רֵעֵיכֶם
	לִבְבוֹתֵיהֶם		רֵעֵיהֶם
	לִבּוֹתֵיהֶם		רֵעָם

2. Draw a line connecting each of the following singular verb forms with the corresponding plural verb form. Identify the root of the singular verb on each line and whether the example given is a perfect, imperfect, or participle form.

Form	Root	Plural	Singular
_____	_____	יָשְׁבוּ	הָיָה
_____	_____	אָמְרוּ	הָיְתָה
_____	_____	בּוֹנִים	יִהְיֶה
_____	_____	אוֹמְרִים	בָּנָה
_____	_____	יוֹשְׁבוֹת	בּוֹנֶה
_____	_____	יֹאמְרוּ	יִבְנֶה
_____	_____	יָדְעוּ	יָשְׁבָה
_____	_____	בָּנוּ	יוֹשֵׁב
_____	_____	יוֹדְעִים	יוֹשֶׁבֶת
_____	_____	הָיוּ	אָמַר
_____	_____	יִבְנוּ	יֹאמַר
_____	_____	יוֹשְׁבִים	אוֹמֵר
_____	_____	יִהְיוּ	יָדְעָה
_____	_____	הָיוּ	יוֹדֵעַ

3. Read and translate the following groups of sentences. Remember that the prefix *vav* can reverse the tense of a verb. Check your translations against those that follow.

.a הָאִישׁ בָּנָה בַּיִת לְמִשְׁפַּחְתּוֹ.
_____

הָאֲנָשִׁים בָּנוּ בָתִּים לַאֲחֵיהֶם וּלְמִשְׁפְּחוֹתֵיהֶם.
_____

_____

וַיִּבְנוּ הָאֲנָשִׁים בַּיִת גָּדוֹל מֵאֲבָנִים גְּדוֹלוֹת.
_____

_____

יִבְנוּ מִשְׁפְּחוֹתֵיכֶם אֶת בָּתֵּיהֶם בְּעִיר הַקֹּדֶשׁ. _____

_____

b. עֶרֶב וָבֹקֶר יָשְׁבָה הַחוֹלָה בַּחֹשֶׁךְ. _____

_____

הַחוֹלִים יָשְׁבוּ בְּבָתֵּיהֶם וְלֹא יָצְאוּ מִשָּׁם. _____

_____

וַיֵּשְׁבוּ הַבָּנִים כָּל חַיֵּיהֶם בֵּין אִמּוֹתֵיהֶם וַאֲבוֹתֵיהֶם. _____

_____

בֵּן אֶחָד לֹא יָשַׁב בֵּין אֶחָיו. _____

c. יוֹם וָלַיְלָה אוֹכֵל הָאָדָם אֶת לַחְמוֹ. _____

_____

יוֹם וָלַיְלָה יַעַבְדוּ הָעֲבָדִים לְלַחְמָם. _____

_____

עֶבֶד אֶחָד לֹא יַעֲבֹד וְלֹא יֹאכַל. _____

_____

עַבְדֵי הָאָדוֹן יֹאכְלוּ אֶת לַחְמָם בְּשָׁלוֹם. _____

_____

d. וַיִּשְׁמַע אִישׁ אֶת קוֹל רֵעֵהוּ. _____

_____

וַתִּשְׁמַע הָאִשָּׁה אֶת קוֹל נִשְׁמָתָהּ. _____

_____

וַיִּשְׁמְעוּ הָאֲנָשִׁים קוֹל שׁוֹפָר בַּדֶּרֶךְ. _____

_____

וְשָׁמְעוּ נְבִיאֵי הָאֵל אֶת קוֹל הַמַּיִם עַל הָאָרֶץ. _____

_____

e. מִי נָתַן לָהֶם גְּבוּרָה? _____

הַמּוֹשִׁיעִים נָתְנוּ לְעַמָּם גְּבוּרָה. _____

_____

הָאֵל הַגָּדוֹל וְהַגִּבּוֹר יִתֵּן אוֹר לְעָם שֶׁהָיָה בַּחֹשֶׁךְ. _____

_____

נֶפֶשׁ אַחַת תִּתֵּן אוֹר לְכָל הָעוֹלָם. _____

_____

Translations

a. The man built/was building/did build/had built/has built a house for his family.

The men/people built/did build/were building/had built/have built houses for their brothers and for their families.

The men/people built/did build/were building a big house from big stones.

May/let your families build {Your family will/may build} their houses in the city of holiness {in the Holy City}.

b. Evening and morning the sick (female) sat/did sit/was sitting/had sat/has sat in the darkness.

The sick ones sat/dwelt in their homes and did not go out from {of} there.

The children/sons dwelt all their lives among their mothers and their fathers.

One son did not dwell/sit among/between his brothers.

c. Day and night the human being/man/humankind eats his bread.

Day and night the slaves/servants will/may work {let the slave/servants work} for their bread.

One slave/servant will/may not work and will/may not eat.

The slaves/servants of the lord/ruler will/may eat {May/let the slaves/servants of the lord/ruler eat} their bread in peace.

d. A man heard/did hear/was hearing the voice of his neighbor/companion/friend/fellow.

The woman heard/did hear/was hearing the voice/sound of her soul/breath.

The men/people heard/did hear/were hearing a sound of a shofar in/on the road/path/way.

The prophets of God will/may hear {Let/may the prophets of God hear} the sound of the water upon the earth.

e. Who gave/did give/was giving/had given/has given to them strength?

The saviors/deliverers gave/did give/were giving/had given/have given to their people strength.

The great and mighty God will/may give {May/let the great and mighty God give} light to the people that were in the darkness.

One soul/mind will/may {May/let one soul} give light to all the world/universe.

Text: Genesis 12:1–7

The first eleven chapters of the Torah present an account of the beginnings of the entire family of humankind. Then the focus shifts to the history of a particular family, the family of Abraham and Sarah, and their descendants, who become the people of Israel. In the beginning of chapter 12 of Genesis, Abraham, charged with his spiritual quest, embarks on his journey.

Read the Hebrew below to see how many of the words you can recognize. This passage does contain words, Hebrew roots, and grammatical concepts that have not yet been introduced. Underline or circle the words, roots, endings, and prefixes that you already know.

¹וַיֹּאמֶר יְהוָֹה אֶל־אַבְרָם לֶךְ־לְךָ מֵאַרְצְךָ וּמִמּוֹלַדְתְּךָ וּמִבֵּית אָבִיךָ
אֶל־הָאָרֶץ אֲשֶׁר אַרְאֶךָּ: ²וְאֶעֶשְׂךָ לְגוֹי גָּדוֹל וַאֲבָרֶכְךָ וַאֲגַדְּלָה
שְׁמֶךָ וֶהְיֵה בְּרָכָה: ³וַאֲבָרְכָה מְבָרְכֶיךָ וּמְקַלֶּלְךָ אָאֹר וְנִבְרְכוּ בְךָ
כֹּל מִשְׁפְּחֹת הָאֲדָמָה: ⁴וַיֵּלֶךְ אַבְרָם כַּאֲשֶׁר דִּבֶּר אֵלָיו יְהוָֹה וַיֵּלֶךְ
אִתּוֹ לוֹט וְאַבְרָם בֶּן־חָמֵשׁ שָׁנִים וְשִׁבְעִים שָׁנָה בְּצֵאתוֹ מֵחָרָן:
⁵וַיִּקַּח אַבְרָם אֶת־שָׂרַי אִשְׁתּוֹ וְאֶת־לוֹט בֶּן־אָחִיו וְאֶת־כָּל־רְכוּשָׁם
אֲשֶׁר רָכָשׁוּ וְאֶת־הַנֶּפֶשׁ אֲשֶׁר־עָשׂוּ בְחָרָן וַיֵּצְאוּ לָלֶכֶת אַרְצָה
כְנַעַן וַיָּבֹאוּ אַרְצָה כְּנָעַן: ⁶וַיַּעֲבֹר אַבְרָם בָּאָרֶץ עַד מְקוֹם שְׁכֶם
עַד אֵלוֹן מוֹרֶה וְהַכְּנַעֲנִי אָז בָּאָרֶץ: ⁷וַיֵּרָא יְהוָֹה אֶל־אַבְרָם וַיֹּאמֶר
לְזַרְעֲךָ אֶתֵּן אֶת־הָאָרֶץ הַזֹּאת וַיִּבֶן שָׁם מִזְבֵּחַ לַיהוָֹה הַנִּרְאֶה
אֵלָיו:

Translating the Torah Study Text

Following is our Torah Study Text, Genesis 12:1–7, reprinted with a literal translation underneath each word. Using your knowledge of the building blocks of the Hebrew language and the meanings of the words provided below, translate this passage into clear English sentences.

Write your translation on the lines following the text. This selection includes some grammatical forms and vocabulary that have not yet been introduced. You will need to rely, in part, on the translations provided.

1 וַיֹּאמֶר יְהוָֹה אֶל־ אַבְרָם לֶךְ־ לְךָ מֵאַרְצְךָ וּמִמּוֹלַדְתְּךָ

said | the Eternal | to | Abram | go | to/for you | from your land | and from your birthplace/kin

---

וּמִבֵּית אָבִיךָ אֶל־ הָאָרֶץ אֲשֶׁר אַרְאֶךָּ:

and from house [of] | your father | to/toward | the land | that | I will show you

---

2 וְאֶעֶשְׂךָ לְגוֹי גָּדוֹל וַאֲבָרֶכְךָ וַאֲגַדְּלָה

and I will make you | [in]to a nation | great | and I will bless you | and I will make great

---

שְׁמֶךָ וֶהְיֵה בְּרָכָה: **3** וַאֲבָרְכָה מְבָרְכֶיךָ וּמְקַלֶּלְךָ

your name | and be | blessing | and I will bless | those who bless you | and he who curses you

---

אָאֹר וְנִבְרְכוּ בְךָ כֹּל מִשְׁפְּחֹת הָאֲדָמָה: **4** וַיֵּלֶךְ

I will curse | and [they] will be blessed | in you | all | families [of] | the earth | [he] went

---

אַבְרָם כַּאֲשֶׁר דִּבֶּר אֵלָיו יְהוָֹה וַיֵּלֶךְ אִתּוֹ לוֹט וְאַבְרָם

Abram | as | [he] spoke | to him | the Eternal | and [he] went | with him | Lot | and Abram

---

בֶּן־	חָמֵשׁ	שָׁנִים	וְשִׁבְעִים	שָׁנָה	בְּצֵאתוֹ	מֵחָרָן:	⁵וַיִּקַּח	אַבְרָם
son	five	years	and seventy	year	with his leaving	from Charan	and [he] took	Abram

אֶת־שָׂרַי	אִשְׁתּוֹ	וְאֶת־	לוֹט	בֶּן־	אָחִיו	וְאֶת־	כָּל־	רְכוּשָׁם	אֲשֶׁר
Sarai	his wife	and	Lot	son brother [of]	his	and	all	their property/ goods	that

רָכָשׁוּ	וְאֶת־	הַנֶּפֶשׁ	אֲשֶׁר־	עָשׂוּ	בְחָרָן	וַיֵּצְאוּ	לָלֶכֶת
they amassed	and	the soul	that	they made	in Charan	and they went out	to go

אַרְצָה	כְּנַעַן	וַיָּבֹאוּ	אַרְצָה	כְּנַעַן:	⁶וַיַּעֲבֹר	אַבְרָם
to the land	Canaan	and they came	to the land	Canaan	and [he] passed	Abram

בָּאָרֶץ	עַד	מְקוֹם	שְׁכֶם	עַד	אֵלוֹן	מוֹרֶה
in the land	until/ as far as	place of	Shechem	until/ as far as	terebinth/ oak	Moreh

וְהַכְּנַעֲנִי	אָז	בָּאָרֶץ:	⁷וַיֵּרָא	יְהֹוָה	אֶל־	אַבְרָם	וַיֹּאמֶר
and the Canaanite	then	in the land	and appeared	the Eternal	to	Abram	and [he] said

לְזַרְעֲךָ	אֶתֵּן	אֶת־הָאָרֶץ	הַזֹּאת	וַיִּבֶן	שָׁם	מִזְבֵּחַ
to your seed/ offspring	I will give	the land	this	and he built	there	altar

לַיהוָה הַנִּרְאֶה אֵלָיו:

to him   who   to the
       appeared   Eternal

Torah Translations

Compare your translation of Genesis 12:1–7 with the Torah translations below.

¹*The* LORD *said to Abram, "Go forth from your native land and from your father's house to the land that I will show you.*
²*I will make of you a great nation,*
And I will bless you;
I will make your name great,
And you shall be a blessing.
³*I will bless those who bless you*
And curse him that curses you;
And all the families of the earth
Shall bless themselves by you."
⁴*Abram went forth as the* LORD *had commanded him, and Lot went with him. Abram was seventy-five years old when he left Haran.* ⁵*Abram took his wife Sarai and his brother's son Lot, and all the wealth that they had amassed, and the persons that they had acquired in Haran; and they set out for the land of Canaan. When they arrived in the land of Canaan,* ⁶*Abram passed through the land as far as the site of Shechem, at the terebinth of Moreh. The Canaanites were then in the land.*

⁷*The* LORD *appeared to Abram and said, "I will assign this land to your offspring." And he built an altar there to the* LORD *who had appeared to him.*

JPS HEBREW-ENGLISH TANAKH: THE TRADITIONAL HEBREW TEXT AND THE NEW JPS TRANSLATION—2D ED. PHILADELPHIA: THE JEWISH PUBLICATION SOCIETY, 1999.

¹*HASHEM said to Abram, "Go for yourself from your land, from your relatives, and from your father's house to the land that I will show you.* ²*And I will make of you a great nation; I will bless you, and make your name great, and you shall be a blessing.* ³*I will bless those who bless you, and him who curses you I will curse; and all the families of the earth shall bless themselves by you."*

⁴*So Abram went as HASHEM had spoken to him, and Lot went with him; Abram was seventy-five years old when he left Haran.* ⁵*Abram took his wife Sarai and Lot, his brother's son, and all their wealth that they had amassed, and the souls they made in*

Haran; and they left to go to the land of Canaan, and they came to the land of Canaan.
⁶*Abram passed into the land as far as the site of Shechem, until the Plain of Moreh.*
The Canaanite was then in the land.

⁷Hᴀꜱʜᴇᴍ *appeared to Abram and said, "To your offspring I will give this land." So he*
built an altar there to Hᴀꜱʜᴇᴍ *Who appeared to him.*

Tʜᴇ Cʜᴜᴍᴀꜱʜ, ᴀʀᴛSᴄʀᴏʟʟ Sᴇʀɪᴇꜱ, Sᴛᴏɴᴇ Eᴅɪᴛɪᴏɴ. Bʀᴏᴏᴋʟʏɴ: Mᴇꜱᴏʀᴀʜ
Pᴜʙʟɪᴄᴀᴛɪᴏɴꜱ, 1993.

¹Yʜᴡʜ *said to Avram:*
Go-you-forth
from your land,
from your kindred,
from your father's house,
to the land that I will let you see.
²*I will make a great nation of you*
and will give-you-blessing
and will make your name great.
Be a blessing!
³*I will bless those who bless you,*
he who curses you, I will damn.
All the clans of the soil will find blessing through you!

⁴*Avram went, as* Yʜᴡʜ *had spoken to him, and Lot went with him.*
And Avram was five years and seventy years old when he went out of Harran.
⁵*Avram took Sarai his wife and Lot his brother's son, all their property that they had*
gained, and the persons whom they had made-their-own in Harran,
and they went out to go to the land of Canaan.
When they come to the land of Canaan,
⁶*Avram passed through the land, as far as the Place of Shekhem,*
as far as the Oak of Moreh.
Now the Canaanite was then in the land.

⁷Yʜᴡʜ *was seen by Avram and said:*
I give this land to your seed!
He built a slaughter-site there to Yʜᴡʜ *who had been seen by him.*

Tʜᴇ Fɪᴠᴇ Bᴏᴏᴋꜱ ᴏꜰ Mᴏꜱᴇꜱ: A Nᴇᴡ Tʀᴀɴꜱʟᴀᴛɪᴏɴ ᴡɪᴛʜ Iɴᴛʀᴏᴅᴜᴄᴛɪᴏɴꜱ,
Cᴏᴍᴍᴇɴᴛᴀʀʏ, ᴀɴᴅ Nᴏᴛᴇꜱ ʙʏ Eᴠᴇʀᴇᴛᴛ Fᴏx. Nᴇᴡ Yᴏʀᴋ: Sᴄʜᴏᴄᴋᴇɴ Bᴏᴏᴋꜱ, 1995.

Now the LORD said to Avram, Get thee out of thy country, and from thy kindred, and from thy father's house, to the land that I will show thee: and I will make of thee a great nation, and I will bless thee, and make thy name great; and thou shalt be a blessing: and I will bless them that bless thee, and curse him that curses thee: and in thee shall all the families of the earth be blessed. So Avram departed, as the LORD had spoken to him; and Lot went with him: and Avram was seventy five years old when he departed out of Haran. And Avram took Saray his wife, and Lot his brother's son, and all their substance that they had gathered, and the souls that they had acquired in Haran; and they went forth to go to the land of Kena'an; and into the land of Kena'an they came. And Avram passed through the land to the place of Shekhem unto the terebinth of More. And the Kena'ani was then in the land. And the LORD appeared to Avram, and said, To thy seed will I give this land: and there he built an altar to the LORD, who had appeared to him.

THE JERUSALEM BIBLE, PUBLISHED FOR THE NAHUM ZEEV WILLIAMS FAMILY FOUNDATION AT HECHAL SHLOMO, JERUSALEM. JERUSALEM: KOREN PUBLISHERS JERUSALEM LTD., 1969.

Vocabulary

Locate each of the following words in the Torah Study Text: Genesis 12:1–7.

year *f*	—	שָׁנָה
Canaan *m*	—	כְּנַעַן
until, unto, as far as	—	עַד
place *m*	—	מָקוֹם
then, at that time	—	אָז
seed, offspring *m*	—	זֶרַע

Notes on the Vocabulary

1. The idiom בֶּן...שָׁנִים (literally, "a son of...years") or בַּת...שָׁנִים ("a daughter of...years") is the Hebrew way of saying "...years old." This idiom appears in our Torah Study Text in verse 4.
2. הַמָּקוֹם, which literally means "the place," is a term used in rabbinic literature for God, the Omnipresent, the One who is in all places.

Hebrew Root Review

In Chapter 10 of *Aleph Isn't Enough,* we introduced a different pattern for forming participles: ▨ ▨ מְ, instead of ▨ ▨וֹ ▨. Six of the roots included in *Aleph Isn't Enough* followed this participle pattern. In this chapter, instead of presenting two new roots, we review those six roots. The following chart is included for enrichment only. This chart presents the regular vowels for each form, but alternate or irregular vowels sometimes appear in biblical texts. It is not necessary to memorize all these participle forms.

MEANING	PARTICIPLE FORMS				ROOT
	f pl	*m pl*	*f sg*	*m sg*	
sanctify, make holy	מְקַדְּשׁוֹת	מְקַדְּשִׁים	מְקַדֶּשֶׁת	מְקַדֵּשׁ	קׁ־דׁ־שׁ
praise	מְהַלְלוֹת	מְהַלְלִים	מְהַלֶּלֶת	מְהַלֵּל	הׁ־לׁ־ל
speak	מְדַבְּרוֹת	מְדַבְּרִים	מְדַבֶּרֶת	מְדַבֵּר	דׁ־בׁ־ר
bless	מְבָרְכוֹת	מְבָרְכִים	מְבָרֶכֶת	מְבָרֵךְ	בׁ־ר־ך
give life, bring to life	מְחַיּוֹת	מְחַיִּים	מְחַיָּה	מְחַיֶּה	חׁ־יׁ־ה
command, order	מְצַוּוֹת	מְצַוִּים	מְצַוָּה	מְצַוֶּה	צׁ־ו־ה

Notice that there are variations caused by the final root letter ה in the last two roots, חׁ־יׁ־ה and צׁ־ו־ה.

The root בׁ־ר־ך appears several times in our Torah Study Text:

(verse 2)

and I will bless you — וַאֲבָרֶכְךָ

(verse 2)

and be a blessing — וֶהְיֵה בְּרָכָה

(verse 3)

and I will bless those who bless you — וַאֲבָרֲכָה מְבָרֲכֶיךָ

(verse 3)

all the families of the earth will be — וְנִבְרְכוּ בְךָ כֹּל מִשְׁפְּחֹת
blessed in you — הָאֲדָמָה

The root ד־ב־ר appears once in verse 4:

And Abram went as the Eternal — וַיֵּלֶךְ אַבְרָם כַּאֲשֶׁר דִּבֶּר

had spoken to him אֵלָיו יְהֹוָה

In verse 1, God tells Abram: לֶךְ־לְךָ. Since the word לֵךְ alone is the command "Go!", why does the word לְךָ ("to you," "for you") also appear?

The emphasis here is on Abraham's quest for himself, for the "root of his own life."
This is the literal rendition of Lekh lekha—*"Go to yourself"; only in the movement inwards is the God-joy that is true life to be found.*

AVIVAH GOTTLIEB ZORNBERG, *GENESIS: THE BEGINNING OF DESIRE*. PHILADELPHIA: JEWISH PUBLICATION SOCIETY, 1995.

A similar idea is reflected in the following song by Debbie Friedman and Savina Teubal, in which the grammatically masculine phrase לֶךְ־לְךָ and the equivalent feminine phrase לְכִי־לָךְ become an expression for the personal journey that each individual undertakes in life.

L'chi lach *[לְכִי־לָךְ] to a land that I will show you*

Lech l'cha *[לֶךְ־לְךָ] to a place you do not know*

L'chi lach *[לְכִי־לָךְ] on your journey I will bless you*

And you shall be a blessing (3x) L'chi lach *[לְכִי־לָךְ]*

L'chi lach *[לְכִי־לָךְ] and I shall make your name great*

Lech l'cha *[לֶךְ־לְךָ] and all shall praise your name*

L'chi lach *[לְכִי־לָךְ] to the place that I will show you*

L'simchat chayim *[לְשִׂמְחַת חַיִּים, "to the joy of life"]*

L'simchat chochma *[לְשִׂמְחַת חָכְמָה, "to the joy of wisdom"]*

And you shall be a blessing, l'chi lach *[לְכִי־לָךְ]*

TEXT: DEBBIE FRIEDMAN AND SAVINA TEUBAL. *THE COMPLETE SHIREINU: 350 FULLY NOTATED SONGS*. NEW YORK: TRANSCONTINENTAL MUSIC, 2001.

God tells Abram to go מֵאַרְצְךָ וּמִמּוֹלַדְתְּךָ וּמִבֵּית אָבִיךָ, "from your land and from your birthplace/kin and from the house of your father." Why are three different locations given when מֵאַרְצְךָ, "from your land," would have encompassed them all?

your land, your birthplace, and your father's house. *But if he has left his land, then of course he has left his birthplace and his father's house. This is geographically backwards. Therefore, the point of this order is not geographical. It is emotional. The three steps are* *arranged in ascending order of difficulty for Abraham. It is hard to leave one's land, harder if it is where one was born, and harder still to leave one's family.*

RICHARD ELLIOTT FRIEDMAN, *COMMENTARY ON THE TORAH*. NEW YORK: HARPERSANFRANCISCO, 2001.

In verse 3, it says וַאֲבָרְכָה מְבָרְכֶיךָ וּמְקַלֶּלְךָ אָאֹר, "I will bless those who bless you and he who curses you I will curse." The first term מְבָרְכֶיךָ, "those who bless you," is plural, while the second מְקַלֶּלְךָ, "he who curses you," is singular.

And I will bless them that bless you, and him that curses you, I will curse.... *A person should try with all his might to have many who like him and few who dislike him, because that is how the world can exist in harmony. We can see this attribute in Abraham, for it states "them that bless you" in the plural, while "him that curses you" appears in the singular.*

RALBAG, AS QUOTED IN *TORAH GEMS*, COMP. AHARON YAAKOV GREENBERG, TRANS. R. DR. SHMUEL HIMELSTEIN. TEL AVIV AND BROOKLYN: YAVNEH PUBLISHING HOUSE, CHEMED BOOKS, 1998.

At the end of verse 3, it states that all the families of the earth וְנִבְרְכוּ בְךָ. This phrase can be understood in various ways: "will be blessed [or 'will bless themselves' or 'will become blessed'] in [or 'with' or even 'through'] you."

all the families of the earth will be blessed through you. *...In some way, at some time, the result of the divine choice of Abraham is supposed to be some good for all humankind. We are never told what this good is supposed to be. Is it that Abraham's descendants are supposed to bring blessing by being "a light to the nations"—setting an example, showing how a community can live: caring for one another, not cheating one another, not enslaving one another, not lending things to each other for profit, and so on and on? Or is it that they are to bring blessing by doing things that benefit the species: inventions, cures, literature, music, learning? It does not say. But at minimum it must mean that the people of Israel do not live alone or apart. Their destiny—our destiny— whatever it is, must be bound up in the destiny of all humankind....*

will be blessed through you. *Rashi takes the plain meaning of this phrase to mean that non-Israelites will bless their children with words such as "May you be like Abraham." His proof for this reading is the wording of Jacob's blessing of his grandsons Ephraim and Manasseh: "Israel will bless with you, saying: 'May God make you like Ephraim and Manasseh' "(Gen. 48:20). But that passage uses an active form of the verb (the Piel), whereas all the occurrences of this phrase in terms of the nations being blessed use forms that are passive or reflexive.... If we take the meaning as passive, then it is as I have translated it here: "the earth's families will be blessed through you." If we take it as reflexive, then it can mean "they will bless themselves through you," which is Rashi's understanding; but a reflexive can also mean "they will get blessing through you." Interpreters are split on this. I believe that the context settles the question. The issue in the story until now has been the course of relations between God and all the families of*

CHAPTER 7   84 *the earth. Now God makes a special bond with Abraham's family and lets him know that this is for the eventual benefit of all families. (See the preceding comment.)*

RICHARD ELLIOTT FRIEDMAN, *COMMENTARY ON THE TORAH*. NEW YORK: HARPERSANFRANCISCO, 2001.

Exercises

1. Make flash cards for each of the new vocabulary words and Hebrew roots introduced in this chapter, or use the flash card set published as a companion to this book. Review the cards to learn all of them.

2. Draw a line connecting each Hebrew word to its English translation. For some words, there can be more than one correct translation.

year	זֶ֫רַע
at that time	
until	עַד
place	
seed	מָקוֹם
as far as	
offspring	שָׁנָה
then	
unto	כְּנַ֫עַן
Canaan	
	אָז

3. The following are singular and plural forms of words introduced as vocabulary in this chapter. Draw a line connecting each plural word to its singular form. Translate both into English.

_____	מְקוֹמוֹת	שָׁנָה	_____
_____	זְרָעִים	מָקוֹם	_____
_____	שָׁנִים	זֶ֫רַע	_____

85   CHAPTER 7

4. Read and translate the following groups of words.

אֶרֶץ כְּנַעַן b.	_____	זַרְעֲךָ	a. _____
מֶלֶךְ כְּנַעַן	_____	זַרְעוֹ	_____
עַם כְּנַעַן	_____	זַרְעָהּ	_____
יוֹשְׁבֵי כְנַעַן	_____	זַרְעֲכֶם	_____
בְּנֵי כְנַעַן	_____	זַרְעָם	_____

בְּשָׁנָה אַחַת d.	_____	מְקוֹמוֹ	c. _____
בְּכָל שָׁנָה	_____	מְקוֹמוֹתָיו	_____
יְמֵי הַשָּׁנָה	_____	מְקוֹמֵנוּ	_____
רֹאשׁ הַשָּׁנָה	_____	מְקוֹמוֹתֵינוּ	_____
שָׁנִים רַבּוֹת	_____	מְקוֹמָם	_____

אָז f.	_____	עַד עֶרֶב	e. _____
מֵאָז	_____	עַד בֹּקֶר	_____
אָז בִּכְנַעַן	_____	עַד עוֹלָם	_____
אָז בָּאָרֶץ	_____	עַד שָׁם	_____
אָז בִּירוּשָׁלַיִם	_____	מֵהָעִיר עַד הַמַּיִם	_____

5. Identify the root of each of the following participles and whether the participle is masculine or feminine, singular or plural. Translate the meaning of the root.

m/f	sing/pl	Translation	Root	Participle
___	___	___	___	מְקַדֵּשׁ
___	___	___	___	מְהַלֶּלֶת
___	___	___	___	מְבָרֵךְ
___	___	___	___	מְחַיֶּה
___	___	___	___	מְחַיָּה
___	___	___	___	מְצַוֶּה
___	___	___	___	מְצַוָּה
___	___	___	___	מְדַבְּרוֹת
___	___	___	___	מְדַבֵּר
___	___	___	___	מְצַוִּים
___	___	___	___	מְבָרְכִים
___	___	___	___	מְקַדְּשִׁים
___	___	___	___	מְהַלְלוֹת
___	___	___	___	מְקַדֶּשֶׁת
___	___	___	___	מְהַלֵּל
___	___	___	___	מְבָרֶכֶת

It is an honor to read from the Torah before one's community in a synagogue service.

Many students of Hebrew are somewhat daunted by the idea of reading from the Torah scroll, since the Hebrew is written without vowels. It may be reassuring to know that virtually everyone, even the most experienced Torah reader, utilizes a special book called a *tikkun lakorim*, תִּקּוּן לַקּוֹרְאִים ("repair/correction for readers" or idiomatically "a guide for precise reading"), as an aid in preparing a Torah reading.

The pages in a *tikkun* are set up in parallel columns. One column shows the Torah passage as it would be printed in a Hebrew Bible, with all the verses marked, vowels shown, and the additional notations called "trope" or "cantillation" marks written above or below the accented syllable of each word, indicating the phrasing and musical motifs for chanting the passage. The second column shows the same passage as it appears in the Torah scroll, in the distinctive handwritten script that includes decorative crowns on certain letters and no vowels or punctuation. Using a *tikkun* enables one who is preparing a Torah reading to practice, self-check, and ensure that the passage is well learned before standing up before the community.

As an example, below is this chapter's Torah Study Selection (Genesis 12:1–7) as it would appear in a *tikkun*:

ויאמר יהוה אל אברם לך לך	וַיֹּ֤אמֶר יְהוָה֙ אֶל־אַבְרָ֔ם לֶךְ־לְךָ֛
מארצך וממולדתך ומבית אביך	מֵאַרְצְךָ֥ וּמִמּֽוֹלַדְתְּךָ֖ וּמִבֵּ֣ית אָבִ֑יךָ
אל הארץ אשר אראך ואעשך לגוי	אֶל־הָאָ֖רֶץ אֲשֶׁ֥ר אַרְאֶֽךָּ׃ וְאֶֽעֶשְׂךָ֙ לְג֣וֹי
גדול ואברכך ואגדלה שמך והיה	גָּד֔וֹל וַאֲבָ֣רֶכְךָ֔ וַאֲגַדְּלָ֖ה שְׁמֶ֑ךָ וֶהְיֵ֖ה
ברכה ואברכה מברכיך ומקללך	בְּרָכָֽה׃ וַאֲבָֽרֲכָה֙ מְבָ֣רֲכֶ֔יךָ וּמְקַלֶּלְךָ֖
אאר ונברכו בך כל משפחת	אָאֹ֑ר וְנִבְרְכ֣וּ בְךָ֔ כֹּ֖ל מִשְׁפְּחֹ֥ת
האדמה וילך אברם כאשר דבר	הָאֲדָמָֽה׃ וַיֵּ֣לֶךְ אַבְרָ֗ם כַּאֲשֶׁ֨ר דִּבֶּ֤ר
אליו יהוה וילך אתו לוט ואברם	אֵלָיו֙ יְהוָ֔ה וַיֵּ֥לֶךְ אִתּ֖וֹ ל֑וֹט וְאַבְרָ֗ם
בן חמש שנים ושבעים שנה בצאתו	בֶּן־חָמֵ֤שׁ שָׁנִים֙ וְשִׁבְעִ֣ים שָׁנָ֔ה בְּצֵאת֖וֹ
מחרן ויקח אברם את שרי אשתו	מֵחָרָֽן׃ וַיִּקַּ֣ח אַבְרָם֩ אֶת־שָׂרַ֨י אִשְׁתּ֜וֹ
ואת לוט בן אחיו ואת כל רכושם	וְאֶת־ל֣וֹט בֶּן־אָחִ֗יו וְאֶת־כָּל־רְכוּשָׁם֙
אשר רכשו ואת הנפש אשר עשו	אֲשֶׁ֣ר רָכָ֔שׁוּ וְאֶת־הַנֶּ֖פֶשׁ אֲשֶׁר־עָשׂ֣וּ
בחרן ויצאו ללכת ארצה כנען ויבאו	בְחָרָ֔ן וַיֵּצְא֗וּ לָלֶ֙כֶת֙ אַ֣רְצָה כְּנַ֔עַן וַיָּבֹ֖אוּ
ארצה כנען ויעבר אברם בארץ עד	אַ֥רְצָה כְּנָֽעַן׃ וַיַּעֲבֹ֤ר אַבְרָם֙ בָּאָ֔רֶץ עַ֚ד
מקום שכם עד אלון מורה והכנעני	מְק֣וֹם שְׁכֶ֔ם עַ֖ד אֵל֣וֹן מוֹרֶ֑ה וְהַֽכְּנַעֲנִ֖י
אז בארץ וירא יהוה אל אברם	אָ֥ז בָּאָֽרֶץ׃ וַיֵּרָ֤א יְהוָה֙ אֶל־אַבְרָ֔ם
ויאמר לזרעך אתן את הארץ הזאת	וַיֹּ֕אמֶר לְזַ֨רְעֲךָ֔ אֶתֵּ֖ן אֶת־הָאָ֣רֶץ הַזֹּ֑את
ויבן שם מזבח ליהוה הנראה אליו	וַיִּ֤בֶן שָׁם֙ מִזְבֵּ֔חַ לַיהוָ֖ה הַנִּרְאֶ֥ה אֵלָֽיו׃

Torah Study Text: Vocabulary and Root Review

This unit's Torah Study Text, Genesis 12:1–7, is reprinted below, highlighting the new vocabulary words as well as the words formed from the Hebrew roots reviewed in Chapter 7. Read this passage again, recalling the meaning of each of the highlighted words or roots.

וַיֹּאמֶר יְהֹוָה אֶל־אַבְרָם לֶךְ־לְךָ מֵאַרְצְךָ וּמִמּוֹלַדְתְּךָ וּמִבֵּית אָבִיךָ אֶל־הָאָרֶץ אֲשֶׁר אַרְאֶךָּ: ²וְאֶעֶשְׂךָ לְגוֹי גָּדוֹל וַאֲבָרֶכְךָ וַאֲגַדְּלָה שְׁמֶךָ וֶהְיֵה בְּרָכָה: ³וַאֲבָרְכָה מְבָרְכֶיךָ וּמְקַלֶּלְךָ אָאֹר וְנִבְרְכוּ בְךָ כֹּל מִשְׁפְּחֹת הָאֲדָמָה: ⁴וַיֵּלֶךְ אַבְרָם כַּאֲשֶׁר דִּבֶּר אֵלָיו יְהֹוָה וַיֵּלֶךְ אִתּוֹ לוֹט וְאַבְרָם בֶּן־חָמֵשׁ שָׁנִים וְשִׁבְעִים שָׁנָה בְּצֵאתוֹ מֵחָרָן: ⁵וַיִּקַּח אַבְרָם אֶת־שָׂרַי אִשְׁתּוֹ וְאֶת־לוֹט בֶּן־אָחִיו וְאֶת־כָּל־רְכוּשָׁם אֲשֶׁר רָכָשׁוּ וְאֶת־הַנֶּפֶשׁ אֲשֶׁר־עָשׂוּ בְחָרָן וַיֵּצְאוּ לָלֶכֶת אַרְצָה כְּנַעַן וַיָּבֹאוּ אַרְצָה כְּנָעַן: ⁶וַיַּעֲבֹר אַבְרָם בָּאָרֶץ עַד מְקוֹם שְׁכֶם עַד אֵלוֹן מוֹרֶה וְהַכְּנַעֲנִי אָז בָּאָרֶץ: ⁷וַיֵּרָא יְהֹוָה אֶל־אַבְרָם וַיֹּאמֶר לְזַרְעֲךָ אֶתֵּן אֶת־הָאָרֶץ הַזֹּאת וַיִּבֶן שָׁם מִזְבֵּחַ לַיהֹוָה הַנִּרְאֶה אֵלָיו:

Building Blocks

Hebrew Verb Patterns

There are several different verb patterns in Hebrew. Until this unit, all the roots introduced in this book followed the same basic pattern for forming participles and for forming imperfect and perfect verbs. While there might be variations caused by certain root letters, such as a final letter הֹ or a first letter י, all the roots still followed essentially the same pattern. The name of this Hebrew pattern is the פָּעַל (paal) pattern. Some call this the קַל (Kal or Simple) pattern.

The names of the other Hebrew verb patterns are derived from the letters פ-ע-ל, the root letters of the Hebrew word for "verb": פּוֹעַל. The name of each pattern, such as פָּעַל, indicates the regular perfect הוּא—"he" or "it"—form for roots in that pattern:

$$ \text{פָּעַל} \; (\blacksquare \underset{\tiny\_}{\blacksquare} \; \underset{\tiny\top}{\blacksquare}) $$

[he] said	—	אָמַר
[he] knew	—	יָדַע
[he] worked	—	עָבַד
[he] sat	—	יָשַׁב

The פִּעֵל (Pi-el) Pattern

The six roots included in this unit, in the Root Review section of Chapter 7, all follow another Hebrew verb pattern: the פִּעֵל pattern. Participles in the פִּעֵל pattern have the prefix מ added before the root letters, and a distinctive voweling pattern, as shown in the chart in the Root Review section of Chapter 7.

All the roots introduced thus far have appeared in either the פָּעַל (paal) pattern or the פִּעֵל (pi-el) pattern. It is possible, however, for a Hebrew root to appear in more than one verb pattern. If the same root appears in both the פָּעַל and the פִּעֵל patterns, it will have a related, but different, meaning in each pattern. The meaning in the פִּעֵל pattern may be an intensification of the פָּעַל meaning. Following are examples from some familiar and unfamiliar roots:

Meaning in פִּעֵל Pi-el	Meaning in פָּעַל Paal	Root
preserve, conserve	guard, keep	שׁ־מ־ר
give life, bring to life	live, be alive	ח־י־ה
desire, covet	love	א־ה־ב
send away, release	send	שׁ־ל־ח
shatter, smash	break	שׁ־ב־ר
teach	study, learn	ל־מ־ד

Perfect Verbs in the פִּעֵל Pattern

The name פִּעֵל indicates the regular perfect הוּא—"he" or "it"—form for roots in this pattern:

$$\text{פִּעֵל (▨ ִ ▨)}$$

[he] praised	—	הִלֵּל
[he] sanctified	—	קִדֵּשׁ
[he] spoke	—	דִּבֵּר

The feminine singular and the plural perfect forms in the פִּעֵל pattern use different vowels but exactly the same endings as the פָּעַל pattern:

▨ ִ ▨—"he" or "it"

ה▨ ְ ▨ָ—"she" or "it"

וּ▨ ְ ▨—"they"

Imperfect Verbs in the פִּעֵל Pattern

Imperfect verbs in the פִּעֵל pattern use different vowels but exactly the same prefixes and endings as the פָּעַל pattern:

י▨ ֵ ▨ְ—"he" or "it"

תְ▨ ▨ ▨—"she" or "it"

וּ▨ ֵ ▨ְי—"they"

Torah Study Text with Building Blocks

Following is an excerpt, Genesis 12:3–4, from this unit's Torah Study Text, reprinted with the two פָּעֵל verbs highlighted. Reread these verses, noting that one פָּעֵל verb is a simple perfect form without prefixes or endings, while the other is a participle with an ending attached. A translation is provided below only for the highlighted פָּעֵל verbs. Remember that there could be other possible translations. For a full translation of the verses, refer back to Chapter 7.

Genesis 12:3–4

³וַאֲבָרְכָה מְ**בָרְכֶיךָ** וּמְקַלֶּלְךָ אָאֹר וְנִבְרְכוּ בְךָ כֹּל מִשְׁפְּחֹת הָאֲדָמָה: ⁴וַיֵּלֶךְ אַבְרָם כַּאֲשֶׁר **דִּבֶּר** אֵלָיו יְהֹוָה וַיֵּלֶךְ אִתּוֹ לוֹט וְאַבְרָם בֶּן־חָמֵשׁ שָׁנִים וְשִׁבְעִים שָׁנָה בְּצֵאתוֹ מֵחָרָן:

those who bless you (מְבָרְכִים with ךָ, "you" ending) —	מְבָרְכֶיךָ
[he] spoke —	דִּבֶּר

GRAMMAR Enrichment

פָּעֵל Pattern

The following charts include the הוּא ("he" or "it"), הִיא ("she" or "it"), and הֵם ("they") forms in the perfect and imperfect for each of the six פָּעֵל roots included in this chapter. These charts present the regular vowels for each form, but alternate or irregular vowels sometimes appear in biblical texts. These charts are included for enrichment only. It is not necessary to memorize these forms. Notice that the irregularities that appeared with final ה verbs in the פָּעַל pattern also occur in the פָּעֵל pattern.

Perfect Forms

"they"—הֵם	"she/it"—הִיא	"he/it"—הוּא	Root	
קִדְּשׁוּ	קִדְּשָׁה	קִדֵּשׁ	ק-ד-שׁ	sanctify
הִלְלוּ	הִלְלָה	הִלֵּל	ה-ל-ל	praise
דִּבְּרוּ	דִּבְּרָה	דִּבֶּר	ד-ב-ר	speak
בֵּרְכוּ	בֵּרְכָה	בֵּרֵךְ	ב-ר-ך	bless
חִיּוּ	חִיְּתָה	חִיָּה	ח-י-ה	give life
צִוּוּ	צִוְּתָה	צִוָּה	צ-ו-ה	command

Imperfect forms

"they"—הֵם	"she/it"—הִיא	"he/it"—הוּא	Root	
יְקַדְּשׁוּ	תְּקַדֵּשׁ	יְקַדֵּשׁ	ק־ד־שׁ	sanctify
יְהַלְלוּ	תְּהַלֵּל	יְהַלֵּל	ה־ל־ל	praise
יְדַבְּרוּ	תְּדַבֵּר	יְדַבֵּר	ד־ב־ר	speak
יְבָרְכוּ	תְּבָרֵךְ	יְבָרֵךְ	ב־ר־ך	bless
יְחַיּוּ	תְּחַיֶּה	יְחַיֶּה	ח־י־ה	give life
יְצַוּוּ	תְּצַוֶּה	יְצַוֶּה	צ־ו־ה	command

Additional Reading and Translation Practice

Translate the following Hebrew excerpts, using the extra vocabulary words provided. Check your translations against the English translations that follow.

1. The Shabbat Candle Lighting Blessing—This blessing is said on Friday evening when lighting the Shabbat candles. The roots ק־ד־שׁ and צ־ו־ה both appear as פִּעֵל perfect forms, with the נוּ ending attached.

to light/kindle	—	לְהַדְלִיק
of	—	שֶׁל

   בָּרוּךְ אַתָּה יְיָ אֱלֹהֵינוּ מֶלֶךְ הָעוֹלָם, אֲשֶׁר קִדְּשָׁנוּ בְּמִצְוֹתָיו וְצִוָּנוּ לְהַדְלִיק נֵר שֶׁל שַׁבָּת.

   _____

   _____

2. From מִי שֶׁבֵּרַךְ—This is the opening phrase of the prayer for healing, said on behalf of those who are ill. The root ב־ר־ך appears in both perfect and imperfect פִּעֵל verb forms. The root ר־פ־א also appears as a פִּעֵל imperfect verb.

the One who {_literally:_ who that}	—	מִי שֶׁ־

מִי שֶׁבֵּרַךְ אֲבוֹתֵינוּ אַבְרָהָם יִצְחָק וְיַעֲקֹב, וְאִמּוֹתֵינוּ שָׂרָה, רִבְקָה,
רָחֵל וְלֵאָה, הוּא יְבָרֵךְ וִירַפֵּא אֶת הַחוֹלֶה\הַחוֹלָה....

_____

_____

3. From וּנְתַנֶּה תֹּקֶף—בְּרֹאשׁ הַשָּׁנָה—This excerpt comes from the second section of the
   prayer recited on Rosh HaShanah and Yom Kippur. A פָּעַל imperfect form of the root ח־י־ה
   ח־י appears in this selection.

it shall be written	—	יִכָּתֵבוּן
fast	—	צוֹם
atonement	—	כִּפּוּר
it shall be sealed	—	יֵחָתֵמוּן
will die, may die	—	יָמוּת

   בְּרֹאשׁ הַשָּׁנָה יִכָּתֵבוּן וּבְיוֹם צוֹם כִּפּוּר יֵחָתֵמוּן.... מִי יִחְיֶה וּמִי
   יָמוּת....

_____

_____

4. Words to Mourners—These words of comfort are traditionally said to mourners at the
   gravesite at the conclusion of the burial service, in their home at the end of a shivah visit
   (condolence call during the first week of mourning), in condolence cards, and when they
   enter the synagogue for Sabbath prayer during the first week of mourning (the shivah period). The new vocabulary word הַמָּקוֹם is used here referring to God.

פָּעַל imperfect from the root נ־ח־ם*, comfort, console*	—	יְנַחֵם
among	—	בְּתוֹךְ
[the] rest, other	—	שְׁאָר
mourner	—	אָבֵל

הַמָּקוֹם יְנַחֵם אֶתְכֶם בְּתוֹךְ שְׁאָר אֲבֵלֵי צִיּוֹן וִירוּשָׁלָיִם.

_____

_____

5. Psalm 148:13–14—These verses are included in the Torah Service before the Torah scroll is returned to the ark. The passage begins with a plural פִּעֵל imperfect from the root ה-ל-ל.

for, because	—	כִּי
exalted	—	נִשְׂגָּב
alone, by itself	—	לְבַדּוֹ
splendor, grandeur	—	הוֹד
He {God} has exalted, aggrandized {_literally:_ raised the horn of}	—	וַיָּרֶם קֶרֶן ל
praise, glory	—	תְּהִלָּה
follower, faithful one	—	חָסִיד
near, close to	—	קָרוֹב

13 יְהַלְלוּ אֶת־שֵׁם יְיָ כִּי־נִשְׂגָּב שְׁמוֹ לְבַדּוֹ הוֹדוֹ עַל־אֶרֶץ וְשָׁמָיִם:
14 וַיָּרֶם קֶרֶן לְעַמּוֹ תְּהִלָּה לְכָל־חֲסִידָיו לִבְנֵי יִשְׂרָאֵל עַם־קְרֹבוֹ הַלְלוּ־יָהּ:

_____

_____

_____

6. Numbers 6:22–26 (Priestly Benediction)—Verses 24–26, the words used in antiquity by the priests (the sons of Aaron) to bless the community of Israel, are now used by parents to bless their children on Shabbat and festivals. This blessing also appears in the traditional _Musaf_ (additional) Shabbat service and festival service, and it is often recited at weddings, circumcisions, and baby-namings. The roots ד-ב-ר and ב-ר-ך both appear in various פִּעֵל forms.

CHAPTER 8

saying	—	לֵאמֹר
speak (*command form from the* root ד־ב־ר)	—	דַּבֵּר
Aaron	—	אַהֲרֹן
so, thus	—	כֹּה
shall you bless (*you pl imperfect from the root* ב־ר־ך)	—	תְבָרֲכוּ
say (*command, from the* root א־מ־ר)	—	אָמוֹר

²²וַיְדַבֵּר יְהוָה אֶל־מֹשֶׁה לֵאמֹר: ²³דַּבֵּר אֶל־אַהֲרֹן וְאֶל־בָּנָיו לֵאמֹר
כֹּה תְבָרֲכוּ אֶת־בְּנֵי יִשְׂרָאֵל אָמוֹר לָהֶם:

_____

_____

פִּעֵל *imperfect from the root* ב־ר־ך *with* ך *ending*	—	יְבָרֶכְךָ
פִּעֵל *imperfect from the root* שׁ־מ־ר *with* ך *ending*	—	יִשְׁמְרֶךָ
may [he] shine	—	יָאֵר
be gracious to you	—	יִחֻנֶּךָ
may [he] raise, lift up	—	יִשָּׂא
and may [he] give, place	—	וְיָשֵׂם

²⁴יְבָרֶכְךָ יְהוָה וְיִשְׁמְרֶךָ: ²⁵יָאֵר יְהוָה פָּנָיו אֵלֶיךָ וִיחֻנֶּךָ:
²⁶יִשָּׂא יְהוָה פָּנָיו אֵלֶיךָ וְיָשֵׂם לְךָ שָׁלוֹם:

_____

_____

7. From אַשְׁרֵי (Psalm 145:9–11, 21 and Psalm 115:18)—These verses are included in the introductory section of the morning and afternoon service. The entire text of אַשְׁרֵי con-sists of Psalm 84:5, followed by Psalm 144:15, all of Psalm 145, and Psalm 115:18.

Psalm 145:9–11

[they] will/may praise you *or* let [them] praise you	—	יוֹדוּךָ
follower, faithful one	—	חָסִיד
יְבָרְכוּ *with* ךָ *ending attached*	—	יְבָרְכוּכָה
glory	—	כָּבוֹד
kingdom, realm	—	מַלְכוּת

⁹טוֹב־יְהֹוָה לַכֹּל וְרַחֲמָיו עַל־כָּל־מַעֲשָׂיו: ¹⁰יוֹדוּךָ יְהֹוָה כָּל־מַעֲשֶׂיךָ
וַחֲסִידֶיךָ יְבָרְכוּכָה: ¹¹כְּבוֹד מַלְכוּתְךָ יֹאמֵרוּ וּגְבוּרָתְךָ יְדַבֵּרוּ:

_____

_____

_____

Psalm 145:21 and Psalm 115:18

praise	—	תְּהִלָּה
my mouth	—	פִּי
flesh	—	בָּשָׂר
we will/may bless *or* let us bless	—	נְבָרֵךְ
now	—	עַתָּה

²¹תְּהִלַּת יְהֹוָה יְדַבֶּר־פִּי וִיבָרֵךְ כָּל־בָּשָׂר שֵׁם קָדְשׁוֹ לְעוֹלָם וָעֶד:
¹⁸וַאֲנַחְנוּ נְבָרֵךְ יָהּ מֵעַתָּה וְעַד־עוֹלָם הַלְלוּ־יָהּ:

_____

_____

Translations

1. The Shabbat Candle Lighting Blessing—Blessed are You, Eternal our God, Sovereign of the universe, who has sanctified us/made us holy with God's {His} commandments and commanded us to light/kindle [the] light/candle of Shabbat.

2. From מִי שֶׁבֵּרַךְ—The One who blessed/has blessed/did bless our fathers Abraham, Isaac, and Jacob, and our mothers Sarah, Rebekah, Rachel, and Leah, may God {He} bless {let God {Him} bless} and heal the *(male)* sick one/the *(female)* sick one....

3. From בְּרֹאשׁ הַשָּׁנָה—On Rosh HaShanah {at the head of the year} it shall be written and on the day of the fast of atonement {on Yom Kippur} it shall be sealed.... Who will/may live and who will/may die....

4. Words to Mourners—May God {the Place, the Omnipresent, the One who is in all places} comfort/console you among the other/rest of the mourners of Zion and Jerusalem.

5. Psalm 148:13–14—They may/will praise {Let them praise} the name of the Eternal One, for/because exalted is God's {His} name alone. God's {His} splendor/grandeur is upon land/earth and sky/heaven. God {He} has exalted God's {His} people, praise/glory to [of] all God's {His} followers/faithful ones, to [of] the Children of Israel, a people near/close to him. Hallelujah! {Praise *Yah*!}

6. Numbers 6:22–23—The Eternal One spoke/did speak to Moses, saying: Speak to Aaron and to his sons saying, So/Thus shall you bless the Children of Israel. Say to them:

   Numbers 6:24–26 (Priestly Benediction)—May/let the Eternal One bless you and keep/guard you. May the Eternal One shine God's {His} face toward you and be gracious to you. May the Eternal One raise/lift up God's {His} face toward you and give/place to/for you peace.

7. From אַשְׁרֵי (Psalm 145:9–11)—Good is the Eternal One to all, and God's {His} compassion/mercy is upon all God's {His} deeds/acts/works. All Your deeds/acts/works will praiseYou {Let/may all Your deeds/acts/works praise You} Eternal One, and Your faithful ones will/may bless You {Let Your faithful ones bless You}. The glory of Your kingdom/realm they will/may say {Let them say the glory of Your kingdom/realm}, and Your strength/might they will/may speak {let them speak}.

   From אַשְׁרֵי (Psalm 145:21 and Psalm 115:18)—Praise of the Eternal One let/may my mouth speak {My mouth may/will speak praises of the Eternal One}, and let/may all flesh bless {all flesh may/will bless} the name of God's {His} holiness {God's holy name}, forever and ever. And we will/may bless {Let us bless} *Yah*, from now and unto eternity, hallelujah {praise *Yah*}.

Exercises

1. Using the Grammar Enrichment charts as an aid, draw a line connecting each of the following verb forms to the corresponding pronoun:

הוּא—he   הִיא—she   הֵם—they

Many lines will connect with each pronoun. Identify the root and whether the form is a perfect, imperfect, or participle. Translate.

Translation	Root	Form	Verb	Pronoun
_____	_____	_____	מְקַדֵּשׁ	
_____	_____	_____	מְדַבְּרִים	
_____	_____	_____	מְבָרֶכֶת	הוּא—he
_____	_____	_____	מְחַיֶּה	
_____	_____	_____	צִוָּה	
_____	_____	_____	הִלֵּל	
_____	_____	_____	דִּבְּרָה	הִיא—she
_____	_____	_____	בֵּרְכָה	
_____	_____	_____	קִדְּשׁוּ	
_____	_____	_____	תְּבָרֵךְ	
_____	_____	_____	יְהַלְלוּ	הֵם—they
_____	_____	_____	יְצַוּוּ	
_____	_____	_____	יְחַיֶּה	

2. Read and translate the following groups of sentences. Remember that the prefix *vav* can reverse the tense of a verb. Check your translations against those that follow.

a. הָאֲנָשִׁים יָשְׁבוּ בְּאֶרֶץ כְּנַעַן שָׁנָה אַחַת. _____

_____

הַמִּשְׁפָּחָה יָשְׁבָה בָּעִיר יְרוּשָׁלַיִם שָׁנִים רַבּוֹת. _____

_____

לֹא הָיוּ הָאַחִים בְּצִיּוֹן בְּרֹאשׁ הַשָּׁנָה. _____

_____

וַיְהִי הָאָדָם בַּחֹשֶׁךְ לַיְלָה אֶחָד. _____

_____

b. אֲנַחְנוּ לֹא יוֹצְאִים מִמְּקוֹמֵנוּ. _____

אֵין מָקוֹם לָכֶם בְּאַרְצֵנוּ. _____

מְקוֹם אֲבוֹתֵינוּ הָיָה בֵּין עוֹבְדֵי הָאֲדָמָה. _____

_____

אָז יִהְיֶה שָׁם מְקוֹם זַרְעֵנוּ. _____

c. מִי מְחַיֶּה כָּל נֶפֶשׁ? _____

הָאֵל הַגָּדוֹל יְחַיֶּה אֶת הַכֹּל. _____

רוּחַ הַקֹּדֶשׁ תְּחַיֶּה אֶת הָעוֹלָם. _____

_____

פְּנֵי הַבָּנִים מְחַיִּים אֶת לְבָבוֹת אִמּוֹתֵיהֶם. _____

_____

d. וַיְדַבֵּר הָאִישׁ אֶל רֵעֵהוּ וַיֹּאמֶר: "בֹּקֶר טוֹב." _____

וַתְּדַבֵּר הָאֵם אֶל בָּנֶיהָ וַתֹּאמֶר: "לַיְלָה טוֹב." _____

וַיְדַבְּרוּ הָאָבוֹת אֶל זַרְעָם וַיְבָרְכוּ אֶת מַעֲשֵׂה יְדֵיהֶם. _____

וַיְבָרֶךְ הָאֱלֹהִים אֶת יוֹם הַשַּׁבָּת וַיְקַדֵּשׁ אֹתוֹ. _____

e. הָאָדוֹן צִוָּה אֶת עֲבָדָיו וַיַּעַבְדוּ עַד עֶרֶב. _____

_____

וַיִּשְׁמְעוּ אֶת קוֹלוֹ וְאֶת דְּבָרָיו מִבֹּקֶר עַד עֶרֶב. _____

_____

וְהָיוּ הַדְּבָרִים אֲשֶׁר הוּא מְצַוֶּה בְּרָאשֵׁיהֶם כָּל הַלַּיְלָה. _____

_____

וְעָבְדוּ כָּל הַשָּׁנָה וְאָז הָעָם יְהַלֵּל אֶת בּוֹנֵי הָעִיר. _____

_____

Translations

a. The people/men dwelt/did dwell/were dwelling/had dwelt/have dwelt in the land of Canaan one year.

The family dwelt/did dwell/was dwelling/had dwelt/has dwelt in the city of Jerusalem many years.

The brothers were not in Zion at the head of the year {at/on Rosh HaShanah}.

The man was in [the] darkness one night.

b. We are not going out [of]/from our place.

There is no place for you [pl] in our land.

The place of our fathers/ancestors was among the workers of the earth/ground/land.

At that time/then will be there the place of our offspring {the place of our offspring will be there}.

c. Who gives life to/brings to life every soul/mind/breath?

The great God will/may {Let the great God} give life to/bring to life everything.

The spirit of holiness {the holy spirit} will/may {Let the holy spirit} give life to/bring to life the world/universe.

The faces of the children/sons give life to the hearts of their mothers.

d. The man spoke to his fellow/neighbor and said: "Good morning."

The mother spoke to her children/sons and said: "Good night."

The fathers/ancestors spoke to their offspring and blessed the work/act of their hands.

God blessed the Sabbath day {the day of the Sabbath} and sanctified it/made it holy.

e. The lord/ruler commanded/ had commanded/has commanded his servants/slaves and they worked until evening.

They heard/did hear/were hearing his voice and his words from morning until evening.

And they will be the words that he commands {The words that he commands will be} in their heads all the night.

They will work all the year and then the people/nation will praise the builders of the city.

Torah Study Text: Genesis 22:1–5, 9–12

As a test of faith, the biblical patriarch Abraham is commanded to offer up his son Isaac as a sacrifice. The following verses are part of the narrative known as עֲקֵידַת יִצְחָק, the Binding of Isaac, which is read in synagogues on Rosh HaShanah. Part of verse 5 through verse 8, containing Abraham's parting words to his servants and the dialogue between Abraham and Isaac as they head up the mountain, have been omitted in order to shorten our selection.

Read the Hebrew below to see how many of the words you can recognize. This passage does contain words, Hebrew roots, and grammatical concepts that have not yet been introduced. Underline or circle the words, roots, endings, and prefixes that you already know.

Genesis 22:1–5

וַיְהִי אַחַר הַדְּבָרִים הָאֵלֶּה וְהָאֱלֹהִים נִסָּה אֶת־אַבְרָהָם וַיֹּאמֶר ¹
אֵלָיו אַבְרָהָם וַיֹּאמֶר הִנֵּנִי: ²וַיֹּאמֶר קַח־נָא אֶת־בִּנְךָ אֶת־יְחִידְךָ
אֲשֶׁר־אָהַבְתָּ אֶת־יִצְחָק וְלֶךְ־לְךָ אֶל־אֶרֶץ הַמֹּרִיָּה וְהַעֲלֵהוּ שָׁם
לְעֹלָה עַל אַחַד הֶהָרִים אֲשֶׁר אֹמַר אֵלֶיךָ: ³וַיַּשְׁכֵּם אַבְרָהָם בַּבֹּקֶר
וַיַּחֲבֹשׁ אֶת־חֲמֹרוֹ וַיִּקַּח אֶת־שְׁנֵי נְעָרָיו אִתּוֹ וְאֵת יִצְחָק בְּנוֹ וַיְבַקַּע
עֲצֵי עֹלָה וַיָּקָם וַיֵּלֶךְ אֶל־הַמָּקוֹם אֲשֶׁר־אָמַר־לוֹ הָאֱלֹהִים: ⁴בַּיּוֹם
הַשְּׁלִישִׁי וַיִּשָּׂא אַבְרָהָם אֶת־עֵינָיו וַיַּרְא אֶת־הַמָּקוֹם מֵרָחֹק:
⁵וַיֹּאמֶר אַבְרָהָם אֶל־נְעָרָיו שְׁבוּ־לָכֶם פֹּה עִם־הַחֲמוֹר....

Genesis 22:9–12

⁹וַיָּבֹאוּ אֶל־הַמָּקוֹם אֲשֶׁר אָמַר־לוֹ הָאֱלֹהִים וַיִּבֶן שָׁם אַבְרָהָם
אֶת־הַמִּזְבֵּחַ וַיַּעֲרֹךְ אֶת־הָעֵצִים וַיַּעֲקֹד אֶת־יִצְחָק בְּנוֹ וַיָּשֶׂם אֹתוֹ
עַל־הַמִּזְבֵּחַ מִמַּעַל לָעֵצִים: ¹⁰וַיִּשְׁלַח אַבְרָהָם אֶת־יָדוֹ וַיִּקַּח
אֶת־הַמַּאֲכֶלֶת לִשְׁחֹט אֶת־בְּנוֹ: ¹¹וַיִּקְרָא אֵלָיו מַלְאַךְ יְהוָה

מִן־הַשָּׁמַיִם וַיֹּאמֶר אַבְרָהָם אַבְרָהָם וַיֹּאמֶר הִנֵּנִי: ¹²וַיֹּאמֶר
אַל־תִּשְׁלַח יָדְךָ אֶל־הַנַּעַר....

Translating the Torah Study Text

Following is our Torah Study Text, Genesis 22:1–5, 22:9–12, reprinted with a literal translation underneath each word. Using your knowledge of the building blocks of the Hebrew language and the meanings of the words provided below, translate this passage into clear English sentences. Write your translation on the lines following the text. This selection includes some grammatical forms and vocabulary that have not yet been introduced. You will need to rely, in part, on the translations provided.

Genesis 22:1–5

אֶת־אַבְרָהָם	נִסָּה	וְהָאֱלֹהִים	הָאֵלֶּה	הַדְּבָרִים	אַחַר	¹וַיְהִי
Abraham	tested	and [the] God	these	the things/words	after	and it was

נָא	קַח־	²וַיֹּאמֶר	הִנֵּנִי:	וַיֹּאמֶר	אַבְרָהָם	אֵלָיו	וַיֹּאמֶר
please/ pray	take	and he said	here I am	and he said	Abraham	to him	and he said

אֶל	לְךָ	וְלֶךְ־	אֶת־יִצְחָק	אֲשֶׁר־	אָהַבְתָּ	אֶת־יְחִידְךָ	אֶת־בִּנְךָ
to	to/for you	and go	Isaac	whom	you love	your only one	your son

אֲשֶׁר	הֶהָרִים	אַחַד	עַל	לְעֹלָה	שָׁם	וְהַעֲלֵהוּ	הַמֹּרִיָּה	אֶרֶץ
that	the mountains	one	on	for an offering	there	and bring him up	Moriah	land

אֶת־חֲמֹרוֹ	וַיַּחֲבֹשׁ	בַּבֹּקֶר	אַבְרָהָם	³וַיַּשְׁכֵּם	אֵלֶיךָ:	אֹמַר
his donkey/ ass	and saddled	in the morning	Abraham	[he] rose early	to you	I will tell

וַיִּקַּח אֶת־שְׁנֵי נְעָרָיו אִתּוֹ וְאֵת יִצְחָק בְּנוֹ וַיְבַקַּע

and he took | two | his lads/young men | with him | and | Isaac | his son | and split

---

עֲצֵי עֹלָה וַיָּקָם וַיֵּלֶךְ אֶל־ הַמָּקוֹם אֲשֶׁר־ אָמַר־ לוֹ

wood | offering | and arose | and went | to/toward | the place | that | [he] said | to him

---

הָאֱלֹהִים: ⁴בַּיּוֹם הַשְּׁלִישִׁי וַיִּשָּׂא אַבְרָהָם אֶת־עֵינָיו וַיַּרְא

God | on the day | the third | [he] lifted | Abraham | his eyes | and saw

---

אֶת־הַמָּקוֹם מֵרָחֹק: ⁵וַיֹּאמֶר אַבְרָהָם אֶל־ נְעָרָיו

the place | from afar | and [he] said | Abraham | to | his lads/young men

---

שְׁבוּ־ לָכֶם פֹּה עִם־ הַחֲמוֹר....

sit | yourselves | here | with | the donkey/ass

Genesis 22:9–12

⁹וַיָּבֹאוּ אֶל־ הַמָּקוֹם אֲשֶׁר אָמַר־ לוֹ הָאֱלֹהִים וַיִּבֶן שָׁם

and they came | to | the place | that | [he] said | to him | God | and [he] built | there

---

אַבְרָהָם אֶת־הַמִּזְבֵּחַ וַיַּעֲרֹךְ אֶת־הָעֵצִים וַיַּעֲקֹד אֶת־יִצְחָק בְּנוֹ

Abraham | the altar | and [he] arranged | the wood | and [he] bound | Isaac | his son

וַיָּ֤שֶׂם אֹתוֹ֙ עַל־הַמִּזְבֵּ֔חַ מִמַּ֖עַל לָעֵצִ֑ים ¹⁰וַיִּשְׁלַ֤ח אַבְרָהָם֙

| and placed | on | him | the altar | on top of | [to] the wood | [he] stretched out | Abraham |

אֶת־יָד֔וֹ וַיִּקַּ֖ח אֶת־הַֽמַּאֲכֶ֑לֶת לִשְׁחֹ֖ט אֶת־בְּנֽוֹ׃ ¹¹וַיִּקְרָ֨א אֵלָ֜יו

| his hand | and took | the knife | to slaughter/ slay | his son | and called | to him |

מַלְאַ֤ךְ יְהֹוָה֙ מִן־הַשָּׁמַ֔יִם וַיֹּ֖אמֶר אַבְרָהָ֣ם אַבְרָהָ֑ם וַיֹּ֖אמֶר

| angel | the Eternal | from | the heavens | and said | Abraham | Abraham | and he said |

הִנֵּֽנִי׃ ¹²וַיֹּ֗אמֶר אַל־תִּשְׁלַ֤ח יָֽדְךָ֙ אֶל־הַנַּ֔עַר....

| here I am | and he said | do not | stretch out | your hand | toward/ against | the lad |

Compare your translation of Genesis 22:1–5, 9–12 with the Torah translations below. Remember that part of verse 5 through verse 8, containing Abraham's parting words to his servants and the dialogue between Abraham and Isaac as they head up the mountain, were omitted from our Torah Study Text in order to shorten the selection. These verses are, however, included in the English translations that follow.

¹Some time afterward, God put Abraham to the test. He said to him, "Abraham," and he answered, "Here I am." ²And He said, "Take your son, your favored one, Isaac, whom you love, and go to the land of Moriah, and offer him there as a burnt offering on one of the heights that I will point out to you." ³So early next morning, Abraham saddled his ass and took with him two of his servants and his son Isaac. He split the wood for the burnt offering, and he set out for the place of which God had told him. ⁴On the third day Abraham looked up and saw the place from afar. ⁵Then Abraham said to his servants, "You stay here with the ass. The boy and I will go up there; we will worship and we will return to you."

⁶*Abraham took the wood for the burnt offering and put it on his son Isaac. He him-self took the firestone and the knife; and the two walked off together.* ⁷*Then Isaac said to his father Abraham, "Father!" And he answered, "Yes, my son." And he said, "Here are the firestone and the wood; but where is the sheep for the burnt offering?"* ⁸*And Abraham said, "God will see to the sheep for His burnt offering, my son." And the two of them walked on together.*

⁹*They arrived at the place of which God had told him. Abraham built an altar there; he laid out the wood; he bound his son Isaac; he laid him on the altar, on top of the wood.* ¹⁰*And Abraham picked up the knife to slay his son.* ¹¹*Then an angel of the LORD called to him from heaven: "Abraham! Abraham!" And he answered, "Here I am."* ¹²*And he said, "Do not raise your hand against the boy...."*

JPS Hebrew-English Tanakh: The Traditional Hebrew Text and the New JPS Translation—2d Ed. Philadelphia: The Jewish Publication Society, 1999.

¹*And it happened after these things that God tested Abraham and said to him, "Abraham," and he replied, "Here I am."*

²*And He said, "Please take your son, your only one, whom you love—Isaac—and go to the land of Moriah; bring him up there as an offering upon one of the mountains which I shall tell you."*

³*So Abraham woke up early in the morning and he saddled his donkey; he took his two young men with him and Isaac, his son; he split the wood for the offering, and stood up and went to the place of which God had spoken to him.*

⁴*On the third day, Abraham raised his eyes and perceived the place from afar.* ⁵*And Abraham said to his young men, "Stay here by yourselves with the donkey, while I and the lad will go yonder; we will worship and we will return to you."*

⁶*And Abraham took the wood for the offering, and placed it on Isaac, his son. He took in his hand the fire and the knife, and the two of them went together.* ⁷*Then Isaac spoke to Abraham his father and said, "Father—"*

And he said, "Here I am, my son."

And he said, "Here are the fire and the wood, but where is the lamb for the offering?"

⁸*And Abraham said, "God will seek out for Himself the lamb for the offering, my son." And the two of them went on together.*

⁹*They arrived at the place of which God had spoken to him; Abraham built the altar there, and arranged the wood; he bound Isaac, his son, and placed him on the altar atop the wood.* ¹⁰*Abraham stretched out his hand, and took the knife to slaughter his son.*

¹¹*And an angel of HASHEM called to him from heaven, and said, "Abraham! Abraham!"*

And he said, "Here I am."

[12]And he said, "Do not stretch out your hand against the lad...."

THE CHUMASH, ARTSCROLL SERIES, STONE EDITION. BROOKLYN: MESORAH PUBLICATIONS, 1993.

[1]Now after these events it was

that God tested Avraham

and said to him:

Avraham!

He said:

Here I am.

[2]He said:

Pray take your son,

your only-one,

whom you love,

Yitzhak,

and go-you-forth to the land of Moriyya/Seeing,

and offer him up there as an offering-up

upon one of the mountains

that I will tell you of.

[3]Avraham started-early in the morning,

he saddled his donkey,

he took his two serving-lads with him and Yitzhak his son,

he split wood for the offering-up

and arose and went to the place that God had told him of.

[4]On the third day Avraham lifted up his eyes

and saw the place from afar.

[5]Avraham said to his lads:

You stay here with the donkey,

and I and the lad will go yonder,

we will bow down and then return to you.

[6]Avraham took the wood for the offering-up,

he placed them upon Yitzhak his son,

in his hand he took the fire and the knife.

Thus the two of them went together.

[7]Yitzhak said to Avraham his father, he said:

Father!

He said:

---

107   CHAPTER 9

Here I am, my son.

He said:

Here are the fire and the wood,

but where is the lamb for the offering-up?

⁸Avraham said:

God will see-for-himself to the lamb for the offering-up,

my son.

Thus the two of them went together.

⁹They came to the place that God had told him of;

there Avraham built the slaughter-site

and arranged the wood

and bound Yitzhak his son

and placed him on the slaughter-site atop the wood.

¹⁰Avraham stretched out his hand,

he took the knife to slay his son.

¹¹But YHWH's messenger called to him from heaven

and said:

Avraham! Avraham!

He said:

Here I am.

¹²He said:

Do not stretch out your hand against the lad....

THE FIVE BOOKS OF MOSES: A NEW TRANSLATION WITH INTRODUCTIONS, COMMENTARY, AND NOTES BY EVERETT FOX. NEW YORK: SCHOCKEN BOOKS, 1995.

And it came to pass after these things, that GOD did test Avraham, and said to him, Avraham: and he said, Here I am! And he said, Take now thy son, thy only son Yizhaq, whom thou lovest, and get thee into the land of Moriyya; and offer him there for a burnt offering upon one of the mountains which I will tell thee of. And Avraham rose up early in the morning, and saddled his ass, and took two of his young men with him, and Yizhaq his son, and broke up the wood for the burnt offering, and rose up, and went to the place of which GOD had told him. Then on the third day Avraham lifted up his eyes, and saw the place afar off. And Avraham said to his young men, stay here with the ass; and I and the lad will go yonder and prostrate ourselves, and come again to you. And Avraham took the wood of the burnt offering, and laid it upon Yizhaq his son; and he took the fire in his hand, and the knife; and they went both of them together. And Yizhaq spoke to Avraham his father, and said, My father: and he said, Here I am, my son. And he said, Behold the fire and the wood: but where is the lamb for a burnt offering? And Avraham said, My son, GOD will provide himself a lamb for a burnt offering: so they went both of them together. And they came to the place which GOD had told him of; and Avraham built an altar there, and laid the wood in order, and bound Yizḥaq his son, and laid him on the altar upon the wood. And Avraham stretched out his hand, and took the knife to slay his son. And an angel of the LORD called to him out of heaven, and said, Avraham, Avraham: and he said, Here I am. And he said, Lay not thy hand upon the lad....

THE JERUSALEM BIBLE, PUBLISHED FOR THE NAHUM ZEEV WILLIAMS FAMILY
FOUNDATION AT HECHAL SHLOMO, JERUSALEM. JERUSALEM: KOREN PUBLISHERS
JERUSALEM LTD., 1969.

Vocabulary

Locate each of the following words in the Torah Study Text: Genesis 22:1–5, 9–12.

behold, here [is]!	—	הִנֵּה
mountain, mount *m*	—	הַר
with	—	עִם
tree, wood *m*	—	עֵץ
eye *f*	—	עַיִן
lad, youth, young man *m*	—	נַעַר

Notes on the Vocabulary:

1. The word הִנֵּה can have pronoun endings attached, as in verses 1 and 11 of our Torah Study Text: הִנֵּנִי, "Behold me!" or "Here I am!"
2. As with other Hebrew prepositions, the word עִם has endings attached when it is followed by a pronoun such as "them" or "us" or "him":

with them	—	עִמָּם
with us	—	עִמָּנוּ
with him	—	עִמּוֹ

The basic meaning of the root ע־ל־ה is "go up" or "ascend." This root follows the פָּעַל pattern, with the usual variations caused by the final root letter ה. The root ע־ל־ה also follows another verb pattern that will be introduced in Chapter 10. The following are the four פָּעַל participle forms:

$$\text{m sg} \ \ \text{עוֹלֶה} \quad \text{f sg} \ \ \text{עוֹלָה} \quad \text{m pl} \ \ \text{עוֹלִים} \quad \text{f pl} \ \ \text{עוֹלוֹת}$$

The perfect and imperfect forms can be found in the verb charts in the back of the book.

In this chapter's Torah Study Text, the root ע־ל־ה appears in verse 3 as the word עֹלָה, referring to a type of animal sacrifice in which the offering was completely consumed, "going up" in the flames of the altar.

(verse 3)

he split [the] wood of [the] offering   —   וַיְבַקַּע עֲצֵי עֹלָה

In verse 2, the root ע־ל־ה appears as both the word עֹלָה and as a verb with the הוּ pronoun ending attached:

(verse 2)

and bring him up there for an offering —   וְהַעֲלֵהוּ שָׁם לְעֹלָה

The following words, both ancient and modern, are derived from the root ע־ל־ה. The final root letter ה drops out in some words formed from this root.

whole burnt offering *(a type of animal sacrifice)* —	עֹלָה
high, exalted, supreme —	עֶלְיוֹן
rise, ascent, slope —	מַעֲלֶה
step, stair, degree —	מַעֲלָה
elevator, lift —	מַעֲלִית
from above, above, upon —	מִמַּעַל
upwards, above —	לְמַעְלָה
rising, ascent; immigration to Israel; the honor of being called to the Torah —	עֲלִיָּה
genius, prodigy —	עִלּוּי
El Al, Israel's national airline ("to above") —	אֶל עַל

The basic meaning of the root הָ־ל־ךְ is "walk" or "go." This root follows the פָּעַל pattern, as well as another verb pattern that will be introduced in Chapter 10. The following are the four פָּעַל participle forms:

f pl הוֹלְכוֹת   *m pl* הוֹלְכִים   *f sg* הוֹלֶכֶת   *m sg* הוֹלֵךְ

The perfect and imperfect forms can be found in the verb charts in the back of the book.

The root הָ־ל־ךְ appears twice in our Torah Study Text. The first root letter הַ has dropped out in both these examples:

(verse 2)

and go to/for you to the land of
Moriah — וְלֶךְ־לְךָ אֶל־אֶרֶץ הַמֹּרִיָּה

(verse 3)

and went to/toward the place — וַיֵּלֶךְ אֶל־הַמָּקוֹם

The following words, both ancient and modern, are derived from the root הָ־ל־ךְ. The first root letter הַ drops out in some words formed from this root.

law, rule, tradition, *halachah* (Jewish law) —	הֲלָכָה
custom, practice —	הָלִיךְ
walking, conduct, manners —	הֲלִיכָה
there and back, going and returning, round trip —	הָלוֹךְ וָשׁוֹב
traveler, wanderer, wayfarer —	הֵלֶךְ
walking, journey, distance, move *(as in chess)*, stroke *(of an engine)* —	מַהֲלָךְ
promenade —	מַהֲלָכָה
procession —	תַּהֲלוּכָה
process —	תַּהֲלִיךְ

Commentary

What could possibly have prompted God to devise a test of faith such as עֲקֵידַת יִצְחָק, the Binding of Isaac? The first verse states וַיְהִי אַחַר הַדְּבָרִים הָאֵלֶה, "and it was after these דְּבָרִים," which can mean either "things" or "words." The following midrash uses this double meaning of דְּבָרִים to link this test of faith to the preceding chapter (Genesis 21) and the rivalry between Isaac and his older half-brother Ishmael. By viewing דְּבָרִים as words exchanged between the brothers, this midrash also transforms Isaac's role from that of an innocent victim to a willing participant.

וַיְהִי אַחַר הַדְּבָרִים הָאֵלֶה וְהָאֱלֹהִים נִסָּה אֶת־אַבְרָהָם, **And it was after these things/words and God tested Abraham.** And what words were there? It was that Ishmael had said to Isaac, "I am greater than you, for I was circumcised when I was thirteen years old and I endured the pain, but you were circumcised when you were eight days old and didn't know any pain. Even if your father had slaughtered you, you wouldn't have known it. If you had been thirteen years old, you wouldn't have taken the pain." Isaac said to him, "That's nothing! If the blessed Holy One said to my father: 'Slaughter Isaac your son!', I wouldn't refuse." At once, the matter דָּבָר (word/thing) sprung upon God, as it is said, "And it was after these things/words and God tested Abraham."

TANCHUMA, VAYEIRA 18

How could God command such an act as the slaughter of one's own child? The following commentary notes that the verb הַעֲלֵהוּ in verse 2 could be understood simply as "bring him up" and not necessarily as "offer him up."

וְהַעֲלֵהוּ, **And bring him up.** God did not say, "Slaughter him," because the blessed Holy One did not desire that he slaughter him, but rather that he bring him up on the mountain to make him an Olah [i.e., to prepare him for sacrifice without actually doing it]. And once he brought him up, God said to him, "Bring him down."

RASHI ON GENESIS 22:2

The Torah does not record Abraham's reply to God's command, only his actions. Did Abraham protest? How did he feel? The following two excerpts give us different portrayals of Abraham's response. In the first, from a song by Bob Dylan, a conversation of protest and coercion between Abraham and God is imagined. In the second, a Chasidic commentary, the double meaning of the word הַמָּקוֹם in verse 4 ("the place/the One who is in all places") provides an insight into Abraham's spiritual state.

> God said to Abraham, "Kill me a son."
> Abe said to God, "You must be puttin' me on!"
> God said, "No." Abe said, "What!"
> God said, "You can do what you want to, but...
> next time you see me coming, you'd better run!"

Abe said, "Where d'ya want this killing done?"
God said, "Out on Highway 61."

FROM "HIGHWAY 61," BY BOB DYLAN

וַיַּרְא אֶת־הַמָּקוֹם מֵרָחֹק, **and saw the place from afar.** The word "place" *(הַמָּקוֹם)*
is often used as a synonym for God. In other words, Abraham saw God from afar off, and
not from close by as was normal for him....

R' AVRAHAM OF SOCHACHEW, AS QUOTED IN *TORAH GEMS*, COMP. AHARON YAAKOV
GREENBERG, TRANS. R. DR. SHMUEL HIMELSTEIN. TEL AVIV AND BROOKLYN: YAVNEH
PUBLISHING HOUSE, CHEMED BOOKS, 1998.

Sarah is conspicuously absent from this story. It is difficult to imagine that Isaac's mother would
have had nothing to say about Abraham's plans as he took Isaac away. The following classical
midrash envisions Sarah and her potential objections as the reason behind the words in verse 3:
וַיַּשְׁכֵּם אַבְרָהָם בַּבֹּקֶר, "Abraham rose early in the morning."

Abraham said: "What shall I do? If I tell Sarah—women get upset over a small thing, all
the more so over a big thing like this! But if I don't tell her, and I steal him away from
her, when she doesn't see him, she'll kill herself." What did he do? He said to Sarah,
"Prepare us food and drink, and let's eat and rejoice!" She said to him, "What's so spe-
cial about today, and what type of celebration is this?" He said to her, "Old people like
ourselves with a son born to them in their old age—it's fitting to eat and drink and be
happy!" She went and she prepared the food. When they were in the midst of the meal,
he said to her, "You know when I was three years old, I met my Creator, and this lad is
grown and he hasn't been educated. There's a place somewhat far from us where they
educate the young men; let me take him and educate him there." She said to him, "Go
in peace." At once וַיַּשְׁכֵּם אַבְרָהָם בַּבֹּקֶר, *"Abraham rose early in the morning."*
And why in the morning? He said, "Perhaps Sarah will go back on her word and won't
permit me [to go with Isaac]. I'll get up early before she gets up."

TANCHUMA, VAYEIRA 22

Exercises

1. Make flash cards for each of the new vocabulary words and Hebrew roots introduced in this chapter, or use the flash card set published as a companion to this book. Review the cards to learn all of them.

2. Draw a line connecting each Hebrew word to its English translation. For some words, there can be more than one correct translation.

behold	עֵץ
mountain	
youth	הַר
tree	
lad	הִנֵּה
mount	
here [is]	עִם
wood	
with	עַיִן
eye	
	נַעַר

3. The following are singular and plural forms of words introduced as vocabulary in this chapter. Draw a line connecting each plural word to its singular form. Translate both into English.

_____	עֵצִים	הַר	_____
_____	הָרִים	נַעַר	_____
_____	עֵינַיִם	עַיִן	_____
_____	נְעָרִים	עֵץ	_____

4. Read and translate the following groups of words.

b. נַעַרְךָ _____   a. עֵינוֹ _____

נַעַרְכֶם _____   עֵינָיו _____

נַעֲרֵיכֶם _____   עֵינֵינוּ _____

נַעֲרָם _____   עֵינֵיכֶם _____

נַעֲרֵיהֶם _____   עֵינֵיהֶם _____

d. הִנְּךָ _____   c. עִמָּנוּ _____

הִנּוֹ _____   עִמּוֹ _____

הִנֶּנּוּ _____   עִמָּהּ _____

הִנְּכֶם _____   עִמָּכֶם _____

הִנָּם _____   עִמָּם _____

f. עֵץ טוֹב _____   e. הַר הָאֱלֹהִים _____

עֵץ אֶחָד _____   הַר בֵּית אֵל _____

עֵץ וָאֶבֶן _____   הַר צִיּוֹן _____

עֵץ הַחַיִּים _____   הַר הַקֹּדֶשׁ _____

עֵץ פְּרִי _____   רֹאשׁ הָהָר _____

5. Identify the root of each of the following participles and whether the participle form is masculine or feminine, singular or plural. Translate the meaning of the root.

m/f	sing/pl	Translation	Root	Participle
_____	_____	_____	_____	עוֹשָׂה
_____	_____	_____	_____	עוֹלֶה
_____	_____	_____	_____	עוֹלָה
_____	_____	_____	_____	בּוֹנִים
_____	_____	_____	_____	יוֹדְעִים

				יוֹשְׁבִים
____	____	____	____	מְבָרְכִים
____	____	____	____	מְהַלְלוֹת
____	____	____	____	הוֹלֵךְ
____	____	____	____	הוֹלֶכֶת
____	____	____	____	יוֹשְׁבוֹת
____	____	____	____	בּוֹחֲרִים
____	____	____	____	עוֹבְדוֹת
____	____	____	____	מְקַדֵּשׁ
____	____	____	____	מְצַוֶּה
____	____	____	____	אוֹמֶרֶת

The Akeidah and Rosh HaShanah

EXTRA CREDIT

As mentioned at the beginning of the chapter, עֲקֵידַת יִצְחָק, the Binding of Isaac, is read in synagogues on Rosh HaShanah. It is a challenging and disturbing narrative, which has given rise to much commentary over the ages. Questions abound as to why the dramatis personae in this story (whether God or Abraham or Isaac) would act in the manner in which they do, which appears so contrary to our usual notions of morality and justice.

In a traditional understanding of this narrative, Abraham's willingness to offer up to God his most precious, beloved son is viewed as a heroic example of sacrifice in obedience to the will of God. Isaac, too, over the ages became an important symbol of self-sacrifice, of Jewish martyrdom, for his readiness to die in a demonstration of faith.

The selection of this passage for reading on Rosh HaShanah is related to the concept in Jewish thought of זְכוּת אָבוֹת, "the merit of our ancestors," the idea that the good and noble deeds of our ancestors contribute to the well-being of their descendants. The merit of a good deed continues forever, and as our own deeds are evaluated and judged on Rosh HaShanah, the harshness of judgment may be softened or mitigated by the recollection of past good deeds performed by our ancestors.

This thought is reflected in the following midrashic passage, which presents a conversation between Abraham and God after Abraham is instructed to leave his son unharmed:

(Abraham speaking to God:) "...I overcame my impulse [to challenge and refuse Your command] and I didn't reply to You, so when [in the future] the children of Isaac will

sin and come upon affliction, be mindful for them of the binding of Isaac and let it be considered before You as if his ashes were piled up on the altar, and forgive them and redeem them from their affliction."

The blessed Holy One said to him: "You have said your piece, and now I'll say Mine. In the future, the children of Isaac will sin before Me and I will judge them on Rosh HaShanah. And if they want Me to find merit in them and to recall on their behalf the binding of Isaac, they will blow before Me on the shofar of this one."

He asked: "And what is the shofar?"

He said, "Turn around."

Immediately, Abraham lifted his eyes and saw, and behold a ram, behind, caught in the thicket by its horns (Genesis 22:13)....

The blessed Holy One said to him: "They will blow before Me on a ram's horn and I will save them and redeem them from their iniquity."

TANCHUMA, VAYEIRA 22

דָּבָר אַחֵר, "a different interpretation": Many contemporary readers find it difficult to praise the actions of Abraham or to embrace the notion of זְכוּת אָבוֹת, "the merit of our ancestors." Some suggest a contrary reading of the passage: that Abraham failed God's test, in that he did not challenge God's command or argue on behalf of his son. Though God does not withdraw Abraham's blessing, nonetheless God never again speaks directly to Abraham in the Torah.

Torah Study Text: Vocabulary and Root Review

This unit's Torah Study Text, Genesis 22:1–5, 9–12, is reprinted below, high-lighting the new vocabulary words as well as the words formed from the new Hebrew roots introduced in Chapter 9. Read this passage again, recalling the meaning of each of the highlighted words or roots.

Genesis 22:1–5

¹וַיְהִי אַחַר הַדְּבָרִים הָאֵלֶּה וְהָאֱלֹהִים נִסָּה אֶת־אַבְרָהָם וַיֹּאמֶר
אֵלָיו אַבְרָהָם וַיֹּאמֶר **הִנֵּנִי**: ²וַיֹּאמֶר קַח־נָא אֶת־בִּנְךָ אֶת־יְחִידְךָ
אֲשֶׁר־אָהַבְתָּ אֶת־יִצְחָק וְ**לֶךְ**־לְךָ אֶל־אֶרֶץ הַמֹּרִיָּה וְ**הַעֲלֵהוּ** שָׁם
לְ**עֹלָה** עַל אַחַד הֶ**הָרִים** אֲשֶׁר אֹמַר אֵלֶיךָ: ³וַיַּשְׁכֵּם אַבְרָהָם בַּבֹּקֶר
וַיַּחֲבֹשׁ אֶת־חֲמֹרוֹ וַיִּקַּח אֶת־שְׁנֵי **נְעָרָיו** אִתּוֹ וְאֵת יִצְחָק בְּנוֹ וַיְבַקַּע
עֲצֵי עֹלָה וַיָּקָם וַיֵּ**לֶךְ** אֶל־הַמָּקוֹם אֲשֶׁר־אָמַר־לוֹ הָאֱלֹהִים: ⁴בַּיּוֹם
הַשְּׁלִישִׁי וַיִּשָּׂא אַבְרָהָם אֶת־**עֵינָיו** וַיַּרְא אֶת־הַמָּקוֹם מֵרָחֹק:
⁵וַיֹּאמֶר אַבְרָהָם אֶל־**נְעָרָיו** שְׁבוּ־לָכֶם פֹּה **עִם**־הַחֲמוֹר....

Genesis 22:9–12

⁹וַיָּבֹאוּ אֶל־הַמָּקוֹם אֲשֶׁר אָמַר־לוֹ הָאֱלֹהִים וַיִּבֶן שָׁם אַבְרָהָם
אֶת־הַמִּזְבֵּחַ וַיַּעֲרֹךְ אֶת־הָ**עֵצִים** וַיַּעֲקֹד אֶת־יִצְחָק בְּנוֹ וַיָּשֶׂם אֹתוֹ
עַל־הַמִּזְבֵּחַ מִ**מַּעַל** לָ**עֵצִים**: ¹⁰וַיִּשְׁלַח אַבְרָהָם אֶת־יָדוֹ וַיִּקַּח
אֶת־הַמַּאֲכֶלֶת לִשְׁחֹט אֶת־בְּנוֹ: ¹¹וַיִּקְרָא אֵלָיו מַלְאַךְ יְהוָה
מִן־הַשָּׁמַיִם וַיֹּאמֶר אַבְרָהָם אַבְרָהָם וַיֹּאמֶר **הִנֵּנִי**: ¹²וַיֹּאמֶר
אַל־תִּשְׁלַח יָדְךָ אֶל־הַ**נַּעַר**....

Building Blocks

Different Verb Patterns

We have now introduced two different Hebrew verb patterns: the פָּעַל pattern and the פִּעֵל pattern. The same root can appear in more than one verb pattern. When a root appears in either the פָּעַל or פִּעֵל pattern, it generally expresses a simple action: "hear," "speak," "guard," "command." If the same root appears in both the פִּעֵל and the פָּעַל patterns, it will have a related meaning in each pattern.

The הִפְעִיל *(Hifil)* Pattern

In this chapter, we introduce a third Hebrew verb pattern: the הִפְעִיל pattern. Roots that appear in this pattern can have a simple active meaning, like roots that appear in the פָּעַל and the פִּעֵל patterns. For example, the root א־מ־ן, introduced in Chapter 10 of *Aleph Isn't Enough*, appears in the הִפְעִיל pattern with the meaning "trust" or "believe."

When, however, a root appears in both the פָּעַל pattern and the הִפְעִיל pattern, it will generally have a causative meaning in the הִפְעִיל pattern. The following examples are included for enrichment only. It is not necessary to memorize this list.

Meaning in הִפְעִיל	Meaning in פָּעַל	Root
cause to eat, feed	eat	א־כ־ל
cause to go, lead, conduct, bring	go, walk	ה־ל־ך
cause to remember, remind, mention	remember	ז־כ־ר
make known, inform, announce	know	י־ד־ע
cause to go out, bring out	go out	י־צ־א
cause to sit, seat, cause to dwell	sit, dwell	י־ש־ב
make king or queen, crown	rule	מ־ל־ך
put to work, employ	work, serve	ע־ב־ד
cause to ascend, bring up, raise	go up, ascend	ע־ל־ה
make heard, proclaim	hear	ש־מ־ע

Recognizing the הִפְעִיל Pattern

The regular forms of the הִפְעִיל pattern have a prefix letter preceding the three root letters and the יִ vowel between the second and third root letters. Even irregular forms of the הִפְעִיל pattern, including many in this chapter's Grammar Enrichment chart, always have a prefix letter preceding the root letters, but they may not contain the יִ vowel.

Perfect Verbs in the הִפְעִיל Pattern

The name הִפְעִיל indicates the regular perfect הוּא—"he" or "it"—form for roots in this pattern:

הִפְעִיל (הִ◼ִ◼ִי◼)

| [he] made remember, reminded, mentioned | — | הִזְכִּיר |
| [he] made king (or queen), crowned | — | הִמְלִיךְ |

All the perfect forms have the prefix letter ה and the same endings as פָּעַל and פִּעֵל perfect forms:

ה◼ִ◼ְ◼ִיוּ—"they" or "it"   ה◼ִ◼ְ◼ִי◼ָה—"she" or "it"   ה◼ִ◼ְ◼ִי◼—"he" or "it"

Imperfect Verbs in the הִפְעִיל Pattern

Imperfect verbs in the הִפְעִיל pattern use the same prefixes and endings as in the פָּעַל and פִּעֵל patterns:

יַ◼ְ◼ִיוּ—"they" or "it"   תַּ◼ְ◼ִי◼—"she" or "it"   יַ◼ְ◼ִי◼—"he" or "it"

Participles in the הִפְעִיל Pattern

The four participle forms have the prefix letter מ in the הִפְעִיל pattern:

f pl מַ◼ְ◼ִי◼וֹת   *m pl* מַ◼ְ◼ִי◼ִים   *f sg* מַ◼ְ◼ִי◼ָה   *m sg* מַ◼ְ◼ִי◼

Variations

It is important to be aware that there are variations on the הִפְעִיל pattern. Sometimes the vowels may be different and the יִ vowel may not appear, particulary when a reversing *vav* is attached. An example of this appears in this unit's Torah Study Text, in verse 3:

Imperfect (from the root שׁ־כ־ם):

[he] will/may rise early — יַשְׁכִּים

Imperfect with reversing *vav*:

[and] Abraham rose early — וַיַּשְׁכֵּם אַבְרָהָם

There are also variations caused by certain root letters. Sometimes a root letter drops out. A good example is provided by the root י־צ־א. The root letter י is replaced by the vowel וֹ:

cause to go out, bring out — י־צ־א   מוֹצִיא

This participle is well-known from the blessing over bread:

בָּרוּךְ אַתָּה יְיָ אֱלֹהֵינוּ מֶלֶךְ הָעוֹלָם הַמּוֹצִיא לֶחֶם מִן הָאָרֶץ.

Blessed are You, Eternal One, our God, Sovereign of the universe, [the One] who brings out bread from the earth.

Torah Study Text with Building Blocks

Following is an excerpt, Genesis 22:2–3, from this unit's Torah Study Text, reprinted with the two הִפְעִיל verbs highlighted. Reread these verses, noting that both הִפְעִיל verbs do not contain the יִ vowel and one has a reversing *vav* attached. A translation is provided below only for the highlighted הִפְעִיל verbs. Remember that there could be other possible translations. For a full translation of the verses, refer back to Chapter 9.

Genesis 22:2–3

²וַיֹּאמֶר קַח־נָא אֶת־בִּנְךָ אֶת־יְחִידְךָ אֲשֶׁר־אָהַבְתָּ אֶת־יִצְחָק
וְלֶךְ־לְךָ אֶל־אֶרֶץ הַמֹּרִיָּה **וְהַעֲלֵהוּ** שָׁם לְעֹלָה עַל אַחַד הֶהָרִים
אֲשֶׁר אֹמַר אֵלֶיךָ: ³**וַיַּשְׁכֵּם** אַבְרָהָם בַּבֹּקֶר....

and bring him up (הַעֲלֵה, bring up, *command
form with* הוּ, him, *ending*) — וְהַעֲלֵהוּ

[he] rose early — וַיַּשְׁכֵּם

הִפְעִיל Pattern

The following chart includes participle, perfect, and imperfect forms for some roots that appear in the הִפְעִיל pattern. Only the הוּא ("he" or "it") forms are shown. The other forms use the regular prefixes and/or suffixes, as shown above, and can be found in the verb charts in the back of the book. The charts below are presented for enrichment only. They include variant forms, caused by certain root letters such as final ה. The vowels shown are the regular vowels for each form, but alternate or irregular vowels sometimes appear in biblical texts. It is not necessary to memorize the information on this chart.

Imperfect	Participle	Perfect	Root	הִפְעִיל Meaning
יַאֲכִיל	מַאֲכִיל	הֶאֱכִיל	א־כ־ל	cause to eat, feed
יַאֲמִין	מַאֲמִין	הֶאֱמִין	א־מ־ן	trust, believe
יוֹלִיךְ	מוֹלִיךְ	הוֹלִיךְ	ה־ל־ךְ	cause to go, lead, bring, conduct
יַזְכִּיר	מַזְכִּיר	הִזְכִּיר	ז־כ־ר	make remember, remind, mention
יַחֲיֶה	מַחֲיֶה	הֶחֱיָה	ח־י־ה	keep alive
יוֹדִיעַ	מוֹדִיעַ	הוֹדִיעַ	י־ד־ע	make known, inform, announce
יוֹצִיא	מוֹצִיא	הוֹצִיא	י־צ־א	cause to go out, bring out
יוֹשִׁיב	מוֹשִׁיב	הוֹשִׁיב	י־שׁ־ב	cause to sit, seat, cause to dwell
יַמְלִיךְ	מַמְלִיךְ	הִמְלִיךְ	מ־ל־ךְ	make king or queen, crown
יַעֲבִיד	מַעֲבִיד	הֶעֱבִיד	ע־ב־ד	put to work, employ
יַעֲלֶה	מַעֲלֶה	הֶעֱלָה	ע־ל־ה	cause to ascend, bring up, raise
יַשְׁמִיעַ	מַשְׁמִיעַ	הִשְׁמִיעַ	שׁ־מ־ע	make heard, proclaim

Additional Reading and Translation Practice

Translate the following excerpts from the Bible and the prayer book, using the extra vocabulary words provided. Check your translations against the English translations that follow.

1. שֶׁהֶחֱיָנוּ—This blessing is said on the first evening of festivals and for other joyous occasions and special events.

[he] has kept alive (הִפְעִיל *perfect* from the root חֹ־יֹ־ה)	—	הֶחֱיָה
[he] has sustained	—	קִיֵּם
[he] has caused to reach (הִפְעִיל *perfect form*)	—	הִגִּיעַ
[to] this time/season	—	לַזְּמַן הַזֶּה

בָּרוּךְ אַתָּה יְיָ אֱלֹהֵינוּ מֶלֶךְ הָעוֹלָם, שֶׁהֶחֱיָנוּ וְקִיְּמָנוּ וְהִגִּיעָנוּ לַזְּמַן הַזֶּה.

_____

_____

2. Isaiah 52:7—A well-known Hebrew folk song and Israeli folk dance are derived from a portion of this verse. A הִפְעִיל participle from the root שׁ־מ־ע appears twice in this verse. There is also a פָּעַל participle from the root א־מ־ר and a פָּעַל perfect form of the root מ־ל־ךְ.

how beautiful	—	מַה־נָּאווּ
foot, footstep	—	רֶגֶל
one who brings good tidings, bringing good tidings (פָּעַל *participle*)	—	מְבַשֵּׂר
salvation	—	יְשׁוּעָה
your God (אֱלֹהִים *with* יִךְ *f sg ending*)	—	אֱלֹהָיִךְ

מַה־נָּאווּ עַל־הֶהָרִים רַגְלֵי מְבַשֵּׂר מַשְׁמִיעַ שָׁלוֹם מְבַשֵּׂר טוֹב מַשְׁמִיעַ יְשׁוּעָה אֹמֵר לְצִיּוֹן מָלַךְ אֱלֹהָיִךְ:

_____

_____

3. From the קְדֻשָּׁה—This excerpt is from the central core of prayers (the עֲמִידָה) in the Shabbat liturgy. A הִפְעִיל imperfect form of the root שׁ־מ־ע with the נוּ ending appears in this passage. Also appearing here is the noun מוֹשִׁיעַ ("savior/deliverer"), which is actually a הִפְעִיל participle from the root י־שׁ־ע.

in the sight of {*literally:* to the eyes of}	—	לְעֵינֵי
living being (*from the root* ח־י־ה)	—	חַי
I	—	אֲנִי

אֶחָד הוּא אֱלֹהֵינוּ, הוּא אָבִינוּ, הוּא מַלְכֵּנוּ, הוּא מוֹשִׁיעֵנוּ, וְהוּא
יַשְׁמִיעֵנוּ בְּרַחֲמָיו לְעֵינֵי כָּל חָי: אֲנִי יְיָ אֱלֹהֵיכֶם:

_____

_____

4. From the קִדּוּשׁ לֵיל שַׁבָּת—This blessing is said over wine on the evening of Shabbat to sanctify the Sabbath.

vine	—	גֶּפֶן
delighted in	—	רָצָה בְּ
love	—	אַהֲבָה
pleasure	—	רָצוֹן
has bequeathed, caused/enabled to inherit (הִפְעִיל *perfect form* with נוּ, *us*, ending)	—	הִנְחִילָנוּ
remembrance, reminder	—	זִכָּרוֹן

בָּרוּךְ אַתָּה יְיָ אֱלֹהֵינוּ מֶלֶךְ הָעוֹלָם, בּוֹרֵא פְּרִי הַגָּפֶן.
בָּרוּךְ אַתָּה יְיָ אֱלֹהֵינוּ מֶלֶךְ הָעוֹלָם, אֲשֶׁר קִדְּשָׁנוּ בְּמִצְוֹתָיו וְרָצָה
בָנוּ, וְשַׁבָּת קָדְשׁוֹ בְּאַהֲבָה וּבְרָצוֹן הִנְחִילָנוּ, זִכָּרוֹן לְמַעֲשֵׂה
בְרֵאשִׁית....

_____

_____

_____

_____

5. הַבְדָלָה Blessing—This blessing is said on Saturday evening as part of the הַבְדָלָה
("separation/distinction") ritual that marks the conclusion of the Sabbath day and the
beginning of the workweek. The root of the word הַבְדָלָה is ב-ד-ל, and it appears
twice in this blessing as a הִפְעִיל participle.

the one who makes a distinction/ separation	—	הַמַּבְדִיל
not holy, ordinary, secular, workaday	—	חוֹל
the seventh	—	הַשְּׁבִיעִי
six	—	שֵׁשֶׁת

בָּרוּךְ אַתָּה יְיָ אֱלֹהֵינוּ מֶלֶךְ הָעוֹלָם, הַמַּבְדִיל בֵּין קֹדֶשׁ לְחוֹל, בֵּין
אוֹר לְחֹשֶׁךְ, בֵּין יִשְׂרָאֵל לָעַמִּים, בֵּין יוֹם הַשְּׁבִיעִי לְשֵׁשֶׁת יְמֵי
הַמַּעֲשֶׂה. בָּרוּךְ אַתָּה יְיָ, הַמַּבְדִיל בֵּין קֹדֶשׁ לְחוֹל.

_____

_____

_____

6. Genesis 1:4—This passage appeared as part of the Torah Study Text selection in Chapter 1.
A הִפְעִיל imperfect form of the root ב-ד-ל, "separate," appears in this verse with a
reversing *vav*. The יֵ vowel changes to ֵ with the addition of the reversing *vav*.

and [he] saw	—	וַיַּרְא
that	—	כִּי
[he] will separate	—	יַבְדִּיל

וַיַּרְא אֱלֹהִים אֶת־הָאוֹר כִּי־טוֹב וַיַּבְדֵּל אֱלֹהִים בֵּין הָאוֹר וּבֵין
הַחֹשֶׁךְ:

_____

_____

7. From מַעֲרִיב עֲרָבִים—This blessing praising God for bringing on the evening appears in the evening service following the בָּרְכוּ. The root of the word עֶרֶב, "evening," עׁ־ר־ב, is used as a הִפְעִיל participle with a causative meaning: "causing evening," "bringing on the evening."

rolling	—	גּוֹלֵל
away from, from before {*literally:* from [the] face of}	—	מִפְּנֵי
causing to pass, making pass (הִפְעִיל *participle from* *the root* עׁ־ב־ר, pass)	—	מַעֲבִיר
causing to come, bringing (הִפְעִיל *participle from* *the root* ב־ו־א, bring)	—	מֵבִיא
making a separation, distinction (הִפְעִיל *participle from* *the root* ב־ד־ל)	—	מַבְדִּיל
a name of God, sometimes *translated as* God of Hosts	—	יְיָ צְבָאוֹת
living and enduring	—	חַי וְקַיָּם
always, continually	—	תָּמִיד

בָּרוּךְ אַתָּה יְיָ אֱלֹהֵינוּ מֶלֶךְ הָעוֹלָם, אֲשֶׁר בִּדְבָרוֹ מַעֲרִיב עֲרָבִים....בּוֹרֵא יוֹם וָלָיְלָה, גּוֹלֵל אוֹר מִפְּנֵי חֹשֶׁךְ וְחֹשֶׁךְ מִפְּנֵי אוֹר, וּמַעֲבִיר יוֹם וּמֵבִיא לָיְלָה, וּמַבְדִּיל בֵּין יוֹם וּבֵין לָיְלָה, יְיָ צְבָאוֹת שְׁמוֹ. אֵל חַי וְקַיָּם, תָּמִיד יִמְלוֹךְ עָלֵינוּ לְעוֹלָם וָעֶד. בָּרוּךְ אַתָּה יְיָ, הַמַּעֲרִיב עֲרָבִים.

_____

_____

_____

_____

Translations

1. שֶׁהֶחֱיָנוּ—Blessed are You, Eternal our God, Sovereign of the universe, who has kept us alive and has sustained us and has caused us to reach [to] this time/season.

2. Isaiah 52:7—How beautiful upon the mountains are feet/footsteps of one who brings good tidings, proclaiming peace, bringing good tidings of good, proclaiming salvation, saying to Zion: Your God has reigned!

3. From the קְדֻשָּׁה—One is our God, God {He} is our Father, God {He} is our Sovereign, God {He} is our Savior/Deliverer, and God {He} will/may proclaim {let God proclaim} [to] us in God's {His} compassion/mercy in the sight of every living being: I am the Eternal your God.

4. From the קִדּוּשׁ לֵיל שַׁבָּת—Blessed are You, Eternal our God, Sovereign of the universe, Creator of the fruit of the vine. Blessed are You, Eternal our God, Sovereign of the universe, who has sanctified us {made us holy} with God's {His} commandments and delighted in us, and the Sabbath of God's {His} holiness {God's holy Sabbath} with love and with pleasure has bequeathed us {has enabled us to inherit}, a reminder/remembrance of the act of Creation....

5. הַבְדָּלָה Blessing—Blessed are You, Eternal our God, Sovereign of the universe, the One who makes a distinction/separation between holiness and not holy, between light and darkness, between Israel and the nations, between the seventh day and the six days of work. Blessed are You, Eternal, the One who makes a distinction/separation between holiness and not holy.

6. Genesis 1:4—And God saw the light that [it was] good, and God separated between the light and between the darkness.

7. From מַעֲרִיב עֲרָבִים—Blessed are You, Eternal our God, Sovereign of the universe, who with God's {His} word makes evening [the] evenings {causes evening, brings on the evening}.... Creator of day and night, rolling light away from darkness, and darkness away from light, making day pass and bringing night, and making a separation between day and between night, God of Hosts is God's {His} name. Living and enduring God, may God {He} always rule over us forever and ever. Blessed are You, Eternal, the One who makes evening [the] evenings {causes evening, brings on the evening}.

Exercises

1. Using the Grammar Enrichment chart as an aid, identify the root of each of the following הִפְעִיל verb forms. Indicate whether the form is a perfect, imperfect, or participle and whether it is singular or plural and masculine or feminine. Translate.

Translation	sg or pl	m or f	Form	Root	Verb
___	___	___	___	___	מַזְכִּיר
___	___	___	___	___	מַאֲכִיל
___	___	___	___	___	מוֹצִיאָה
___	___	___	___	___	מַשְׁמִיעִים
___	___	___	___	___	מַזְכִּירוֹת
___	___	___	___	___	יַמְלִיךְ
___	___	___	___	___	יַעֲלֶה
___	___	___	___	___	תַּעֲלֶה
___	___	___	___	___	תַּאֲכִיל
___	___	___	___	___	יוֹדִיעוּ
___	___	___	___	___	יַשְׁמִיעוּ
___	___	___	___	___	הֶעֱבִיד
___	___	___	___	___	הֶחֱיָה
___	___	___	___	___	הוֹלִיכוּ
___	___	___	___	___	הוֹשִׁיבָה

2. Read and translate the following groups of sentences. Remember that the prefix *vav* can reverse the tense of a verb. Check your translations against those that follow.

a. אַבְרָהָם הָלַךְ מֵאַרְצוֹ עִם מִשְׁפַּחְתּוֹ.

___

הוּא הוֹלֵךְ עַד אֶרֶץ כְּנַעַן וּמוֹלִיךְ אֶת מִשְׁפַּחְתּוֹ.

___

וַיֵּלֶךְ אַבְרָהָם עַד אֶרֶץ כְּנַעַן וַיּוֹלֶךְ אֶת מִשְׁפַּחְתּוֹ. _____

וַתֵּלֶךְ שָׂרָה עִם אַבְרָהָם אִישָׁהּ וַתּוֹלֶךְ אֶת בְּנֵיהֶם. _____
_____

b. אַתָּה עוֹלֶה אֶל הַמָּקוֹם הַקָּדוֹשׁ וּמַעֲלֶה עִמְּךָ אֶת רֵעֶךָ. _____

הָאִשָּׁה עָלְתָה אֶל עִיר הַקֹּדֶשׁ וְעִמָּהּ הֶעֱלְתָה אֶת זַרְעָהּ. _____

וַיַּעֲלוּ הָאַחִים עַל רֹאשׁ הָהָר וְהֶעֱלוּ אֶת נַעֲרֵיהֶם. _____

מִי יַעֲלֶה עִם הָעָם מִן הַמָּקוֹם אֲשֶׁר שָׁם יָשְׁבוּ? _____
_____

c. בְּנֵי אָדָם יָצְאוּ מִן הָעִיר וְאָז הוֹצִיאוּ אֶת זַרְעָם. _____

בָּרוּךְ אֱלֹהֵיכֶם אֲשֶׁר הוֹצִיא אֶתְכֶם מֵאֶרֶץ מִצְרַיִם. _____
_____

הִנֵּה הָאֶבֶן שֶׁהוֹצִיאוּ הַבּוֹנִים מִן הָאֲדָמָה. _____
_____

וַאֲנַחְנוּ הִנֵּנוּ בַּחֹשֶׁךְ וּמִי יוֹצִיא אֹתָנוּ אֶל הָאוֹר? _____
_____

d. הָאֵם אָכְלָה אֶת הַלֶּחֶם וְהֶאֱכִילָה אֶת בָּנֶיהָ. _____

וַתֹּאכַל הָאִשָּׁה אֶת פְּרִי הָעֵץ וַתַּאֲכִיל אֶת אָדָם. _____
_____

בָּעֶרֶב לֹא הֶאֱכִיל הַמֶּלֶךְ אֶת עֲבָדָיו וְאָז לֹא אָכְלוּ. _____

_____

בָּרוּךְ הָאֵל הַמַּאֲכִיל אֶת כָּל הָעוֹלָם. _____

_____

e. וַיִּשְׁמַע הַנָּבִיא אֶת קוֹל הָאֵל וַיַּשְׁמִיעַ אֶת דְּבָרָיו. _____

_____

וַיִּשְׁמְעוּ הָאֲנָשִׁים אֶת קוֹל הָרוּחַ עַל הַמַּיִם וּבֵין הָעֵצִים. _____

_____

עֵינֵי כָּל הָעָם עַל הַנָּבִיא וְהוּא מַשְׁמִיעַ דִּבְרֵי אֱמֶת. _____

_____

עֵינֵי הַנַּעַר עַל פְּנֵי הָאִשָּׁה אֲשֶׁר אָהַב וַיֹּאמֶר "מִי כָמוֹהָ?" _____

_____

Translations

a. Abraham went/was going/did go/had gone/has gone from his land with his family.

He walks/is walking/does walk {goes/is going/does go} as far as/until the land of Canaan and {causes to go} leads/is leading/does lead his family.

Abraham went/walked {did go/walk, was going/walking} as far as/until the land of Canaan and {caused to go} led/did lead/was leading his family.

Sarah went/walked {did go/walk, was going/walking} with Abraham her husband/man and she {caused to go} led/did lead/was leading their children.

b. You are going up/ascending to the holy place and {causing to go up} bringing up with you your friend/neighbor.

The woman went up/did go up/had gone up/has gone up/was going up to the city of holiness {the Holy City} and with her she {caused to go up} brought up/did bring up/was bringing up/had brought up her offspring.

The brothers went up/did go up/were going up on the top of the mountain and they {caused to go up} brought up/did bring up/were bringing up their lads.

Who will/may go up with the people/nation from the place that there [i.e., where] they dwelt/were dwelling/did dwell/have dwelt/had dwelt?

c. The sons/children of Adam {humankind} went out/did go out/were going out/have gone out/had gone out from the city and then they brought out/did bring out/were bringing out/have brought out/had brought out their offspring.

Blessed is your God who brought out/did bring out/has brought out you from the land of Egypt.

Here is/behold the stone that the builders/the ones who build/the ones who are building brought out/did bring out/had brought out/have brought out from the earth/ground.

And we, here we are/behold us in the darkness and who will/may bring out us to/toward the light?

d. The mother ate/did eat/was eating/had eaten/has eaten the bread and {caused to eat} fed/did feed/was feeding /had fed/has fed her sons/children.

The woman ate/did eat/was eating the fruit of the tree and {caused to eat} fed/did feed/was feeding [the] man/Adam.

In the evening the king/sovereign did not feed/had not fed his slaves/servants and [so] then they did not eat/had not eaten.

Blessed is [the] God, [the One] who feeds/does feed/is feeding all the world/universe.

e. The prophet heard/did hear/was hearing the voice of God and he {caused to hear} proclaimed/did proclaim /was proclaiming God's {His} words.

The men/people heard/did hear/were hearing the sound of the wind upon the water and among the trees.

The eyes of all the nation/people are upon the prophet and he proclaims/is proclaiming/does proclaim words of truth.

The eyes of the young man were upon the face of the woman/wife that he loved /had loved /did love and he said, "Who is like her?"

חֲזַק! חֲזַק!

Whenever the reading of one of the five books of the Torah is completed in the synagogue, there is a custom for the entire congregation to stand and say, "חֲזַק! חֲזַק! וְנִתְחַזֵּק!"—"Be strong! Be strong! And let us be strengthened [or let us strengthen one another]!" These are words of congratulations and encouragement—that we have lived to finish another book of the Torah and that we may be granted the strength as a community to do so again. You have now finished the third of the four books in this Hebrew series. You are to be congratulated for all that you have accomplished. May you be strengthened in your further learning!

Verb Charts

The following charts contain all the verb roots, in Hebrew alphabetical order, introduced in *Aleph Isn't Enough* and *Bet Is for B'reishit*. They are separated according to verb pattern: הִפְעִיל ,פִּעֵל ,פָּעַל. Within each verb pattern, they are separated according to perfect, participle, and imperfect forms. These charts present the regular vowels for each form, but alternate or irregular vowels sometimes appear in biblical texts.

פָּעַל Perfect

they *m/f* הֵם\הֵן	she הִיא	he הוּא	Root	Meaning
אָהֲבוּ	אָהֲבָה	אָהַב	א־ה־ב	love
אָכְלוּ	אָכְלָה	אָכַל	א־כ־ל	eat
אָמְרוּ	אָמְרָה	אָמַר	א־מ־ר	say
בָּחֲרוּ	בָּחֲרָה	בָּחַר	ב־ח־ר	choose
בָּנוּ	בָּנְתָה	בָּנָה	ב־נ־ה	build
בָּרְאוּ	בָּרְאָה	בָּרָא	ב־ר־א	create
הָיוּ	הָיְתָה	הָיָה	ה־י־ה	be
הָלְכוּ	הָלְכָה	הָלַךְ	ה־ל־ך	walk, go
זָכְרוּ	זָכְרָה	זָכַר	ז־כ־ר	remember
יָדְעוּ	יָדְעָה	יָדַע	י־ד־ע	know
יָצְאוּ	יָצְאָה	יָצָא	י־צ־א	go out
יָשְׁבוּ	יָשְׁבָה	יָשַׁב	י־שׁ־ב	sit, dwell
מָלְכוּ	מָלְכָה	מָלַךְ	מ־ל־ך	reign, rule
נָתְנוּ	נָתְנָה	נָתַן	נ־ת־ן	give
עָבְדוּ	עָבְדָה	עָבַד	ע־ב־ד	work, serve
עָזְרוּ	עָזְרָה	עָזַר	ע־ז־ר	help
עָלוּ	עָלְתָה	עָלָה	ע־ל־ה	go up
עָשׂוּ	עָשְׂתָה	עָשָׂה	ע־שׂ־ה	make, do
רָפְאוּ	רָפְאָה	רָפָא	ר־פ־א	heal

שָׁמְעוּ	שָׁמְעָה	שָׁמַע	שׁ־מ־ע	hear
שָׁמְרוּ	שָׁמְרָה	שָׁמַר	שׁ־מ־ר	guard, keep

פָּעַל Participle

The following roots follow the exact same pattern as the regular root א־מ־ר and are not listed in the chart: ע־ז־ר, ע־ב־ד, נ־ת־ן, מ־ל־ך, י־שׁ־ב, ז־כ־ר, ה־ל־ך, א־כ־ל, and שׁ־מ־ר. There is no פָּעַל participle form of the root ה־י־ה.

Feminine Plural	Masculine Plural	Feminine Singular	Masculine Singular	Root	Meaning
אוֹהֲבוֹת	אוֹהֲבִים	אוֹהֶבֶת	אוֹהֵב	א־ה־ב	love
אוֹמְרוֹת	אוֹמְרִים	אוֹמֶרֶת	אוֹמֵר	א־מ־ר	say
בּוֹחֲרוֹת	בּוֹחֲרִים	בּוֹחֶרֶת	בּוֹחֵר	ב־ח־ר	choose
בּוֹנוֹת	בּוֹנִים	בּוֹנָה	בּוֹנֶה	ב־נ־ה	build
בּוֹרְאוֹת	בּוֹרְאִים	בּוֹרֵאת	בּוֹרֵא	ב־ר־א	create
יוֹדְעוֹת	יוֹדְעִים	יוֹדַעַת	יוֹדֵעַ	י־ד־ע	know
יוֹצְאוֹת	יוֹצְאִים	יוֹצֵאת	יוֹצֵא	י־צ־א	go out
עוֹלוֹת	עוֹלִים	עוֹלָה	עוֹלֶה	ע־ל־ה	go up
עוֹשׂוֹת	עוֹשִׂים	עוֹשָׂה	עוֹשֶׂה	ע־שׂ־ה	make, do
רוֹפְאוֹת	רוֹפְאִים	רוֹפֵאת	רוֹפֵא	ר־פ־א	heal
שׁוֹמְעוֹת	שׁוֹמְעִים	שׁוֹמַעַת	שׁוֹמֵעַ	שׁ־מ־ע	hear

פָּעַל Imperfect

they m הֵם	she הִיא	he הוּא	Root	Meaning
יֶאֱהֲבוּ	תֶּאֱהַב	יֶאֱהַב	א־ה־ב	love
יֹאכְלוּ	תֹּאכַל	יֹאכַל	א־כ־ל	eat
יֹאמְרוּ	תֹּאמַר	יֹאמַר	א־מ־ר	say
יִבְחֲרוּ	תִּבְחַר	יִבְחַר	ב־ח־ר	choose
יִבְנוּ	תִּבְנֶה	יִבְנֶה	ב־נ־ה	build

יברא	תברא	יברא	ב־ר־א	create
יהיו	תהיה	יהיה	ה־י־ה	be
ילכו	תלך	ילך	ה־ל־ך	go, walk
יזכרו	תזכר	יזכר	ז־כ־ר	remember
ידעו	תדע	ידע	י־ד־ע	know
יצאו	תצא	יצא	י־צ־א	go out
ישבו	תשב	ישב	י־ש־ב	sit, dwell
ימלכו	תמלך	ימלך	מ־ל־ך	reign, rule
יתנו	תתן	יתן	נ־ת־ן	give
יעבדו	תעבד	יעבד	ע־ב־ד	work, serve
יעזרו	תעזר	יעזר	ע־ז־ר	help
יעלו	תעלה	יעלה	ע־ל־ה	go up
יעשו	תעשה	יעשה	ע־ש־ה	make, do
ירפאו	תרפא	ירפא	ר־פ־א	heal
ישמעו	תשמע	ישמע	ש־מ־ע	hear
ישמרו	תשמר	ישמר	ש־מ־ר	guard, keep

פִּעֵל Perfect

they m/f הֵם\הֵן	she הִיא	he הוּא	Root	Meaning
בֵּרְכוּ	בֵּרְכָה	בֵּרֵךְ	ב־ר־ך	bless
דִּבְּרוּ	דִּבְּרָה	דִּבֵּר	ד־ב־ר	speak
הִלְלוּ	הִלְלָה	הִלֵּל	ה־ל־ל	praise
חִיּוּ	חִיְּתָה	חִיָּה	ח־י־ה	bring to life
צִוּוּ	צִוְּתָה	צִוָּה	צ־ו־ה	command
קִדְשׁוּ	קִדְשָׁה	קִדֵּשׁ	ק־ד־שׁ	make holy

פִּעֵל Participle

Feminine Plural	Masculine Plural	Feminine Singular	Masculine Singular	Root	Meaning
מְבָרְכוֹת	מְבָרְכִים	מְבָרֶכֶת	מְבָרֵךְ	בּ־ר־ך	bless
מְדַבְּרוֹת	מְדַבְּרִים	מְדַבֶּרֶת	מְדַבֵּר	דּ־בּ־ר	speak
מְהַלְלוֹת	מְהַלְלִים	מְהַלֶּלֶת	מְהַלֵּל	ה־ל־ל	praise
מְחַיּוֹת	מְחַיִּים	מְחַיָּה	מְחַיֶּה	ח־י־ה	bring to life
מְצַוּוֹת	מְצַוִּים	מְצַוָּה	מְצַוֶּה	צ־ו־ה	command
מְקַדְּשׁוֹת	מְקַדְּשִׁים	מְקַדֶּשֶׁת	מְקַדֵּשׁ	ק־ד־שׁ	make holy

פִּעֵל Imperfect

they m הֵם	she הִיא	he הוּא	Root	Meaning
יְבָרְכוּ	תְּבָרֵךְ	יְבָרֵךְ	בּ־ר־ך	bless
יְדַבְּרוּ	תְּדַבֵּר	יְדַבֵּר	דּ־בּ־ר	speak
יְהַלְלוּ	תְּהַלֵּל	יְהַלֵּל	ה־ל־ל	praise
יְחַיּוּ	תְּחַיֶּה	יְחַיֶּה	ח־י־ה	bring to life
יְצַוּוּ	תְּצַוֶּה	יְצַוֶּה	צ־ו־ה	command
יְקַדְּשׁוּ	תְּקַדֵּשׁ	יְקַדֵּשׁ	ק־ד־שׁ	make holy

הִפְעִיל Perfect

they m/f הֵם\הֵן	she הִיא	he הוּא	Root	Meaning
הֶאֱכִילוּ	הֶאֱכִילָה	הֶאֱכִיל	א־כ־ל	cause to eat, feed
הֶאֱמִינוּ	הֶאֱמִינָה	הֶאֱמִין	א־מ־ן	trust, believe
הוֹלִיכוּ	הוֹלִיכָה	הוֹלִיךְ	ה־ל־ך	cause to go, lead, conduct
הִזְכִּירוּ	הִזְכִּירָה	הִזְכִּיר	ז־כ־ר	remind, make remember
הֶחֱיוּ	הֶחֱיתָה	הֶחֱיָה	ח־י־ה	keep alive
הוֹדִיעוּ	הוֹדִיעָה	הוֹדִיעַ	י־ד־ע	make known, announce
הוֹצִיאוּ	הוֹצִיאָה	הוֹצִיא	י־צ־א	bring out, take out

			Root	Meaning
הוֹשִׁיבוּ	הוֹשִׁיבָה	הוֹשִׁיב	י־ש־ב	cause to sit, dwell, seat
הִמְלִיכוּ	הִמְלִיכָה	הִמְלִיךְ	מ־ל־ך	make king or queen, crown
הֶעֱבִידוּ	הֶעֱבִידָה	הֶעֱבִיד	ע־ב־ד	put to work, employ
הֶעֱלוּ	הֶעֶלְתָה	הֶעֱלָה	ע־ל־ה	raise, cause to ascend
הִשְׁמִיעוּ	הִשְׁמִיעָה	הִשְׁמִיעַ	ש־מ־ע	make heard, proclaim

הִפְעִיל Participle

Feminine Plural	Masculine Plural	Feminine Singular	Masculine Singular	Root	Meaning
מַאֲכִילוֹת	מַאֲכִילִים	מַאֲכִילָה	מַאֲכִיל	א־כ־ל	cause to eat, feed
מַאֲמִינוֹת	מַאֲמִינִים	מַאֲמִינָה	מַאֲמִין	א־מ־ן	trust, believe
מוֹלִיכוֹת	מוֹלִיכִים	מוֹלִיכָה	מוֹלִיךְ	ה־ל־ך	cause to go, lead, conduct
מַזְכִּירוֹת	מַזְכִּירִים	מַזְכִּירָה	מַזְכִּיר	ז־כ־ר	remind, make remember
מְחַיּוֹת	מְחַיִּים	מְחַיָּה	מְחַיֶה	ח־י־ה	keep alive
מוֹדִיעוֹת	מוֹדִיעִים	מוֹדִיעָה	מוֹדִיעַ	י־ד־ע	make known, announce
מוֹצִיאוֹת	מוֹצִיאִים	מוֹצִיאָה	מוֹצִיא	י־צ־א	bring out, take out
מוֹשִׁיבוֹת	מוֹשִׁיבִים	מוֹשִׁיבָה	מוֹשִׁיב	י־ש־ב	cause to sit, dwell, seat
מַמְלִיכוֹת	מַמְלִיכִים	מַמְלִיכָה	מַמְלִיךְ	מ־ל־ך	make king or queen, crown
מַעֲבִידוֹת	מַעֲבִידִים	מַעֲבִידָה	מַעֲבִיד	ע־ב־ד	put to work, employ
מַעֲלוֹת	מַעֲלִים	מַעֲלָה	מַעֲלֶה	ע־ל־ה	raise, cause to ascend
מַשְׁמִיעוֹת	מַשְׁמִיעִים	מַשְׁמִיעָה	מַשְׁמִיעַ	ש־מ־ע	make heard, proclaim

הִפְעִיל Imperfect

they m הֵם	she הִיא	he הוּא	Root	Meaning
יַאֲכִילוּ	תַּאֲכִיל	יַאֲכִיל	א־כ־ל	cause to eat, feed
יַאֲמִינוּ	תַּאֲמִין	יַאֲמִין	א־מ־ן	trust, believe
יוֹלִיכוּ	תּוֹלִיךְ	יוֹלִיךְ	ה־ל־ך	cause to go, lead, conduct
יַזְכִּירוּ	תַּזְכִּיר	יַזְכִּיר	ז־כ־ר	remind, make remember
יַחֲיוּ	תַּחֲיֶה	יַחֲיֶה	ח־י־ה	keep alive
יוֹדִיעוּ	תּוֹדִיעַ	יוֹדִיעַ	י־ד־ע	make known, announce
יוֹצִיאוּ	תּוֹצִיא	יוֹצִיא	י־צ־א	bring out, take out
יוֹשִׁיבוּ	תּוֹשִׁיב	יוֹשִׁיב	י־שׁ־ב	cause to sit, dwell, seat
יַמְלִיכוּ	תַּמְלִיךְ	יַמְלִיךְ	מ־ל־ך	make king or queen, crown
יַעֲבִידוּ	תַּעֲבִיד	יַעֲבִיד	ע־ב־ד	put to work, employ
יַעֲלוּ	תַּעֲלֶה	יַעֲלֶה	ע־ל־ה	raise, cause to ascend
יַשְׁמִיעוּ	תַּשְׁמִיעַ	יַשְׁמִיעַ	שׁ־מ־ע	make heard, proclaim

Glossary

א

father; ancestor *m (A.I.E. Ch 5)* אָב, אָבוֹת

stone *f (B.I.F.B. Ch 5)* אֶבֶן, אֲבָנִים

Abraham *(A.I.E. Ch 5)* אַבְרָהָם

lord, ruler *m (A.I.E. Ch 7)* אָדוֹן, אֲדוֹנִים

human being, man, humankind *m (B.I.F.B. Ch 3)* אָדָם

earth, ground, land *f (A.I.E. Ch 8)* אֲדָמָה, אֲדָמוֹת

love *(A.I.E. Ch 6)* א־ה־ב (פָּעַל)

light *m (B.I.F.B. Ch 1)* אוֹר, אוֹרִים & אוֹרוֹת

then, at that time *(B.I.F.B. Ch 7)* אָז

brother *m (B.I.F.B. Ch 3)* אָח, אַחִים

one *m (plural: a few, some) (B.I.F.B. Ch 5)* אֶחָד, אֲחָדִים

one *f (plural: a few, some) (B.I.F.B. Ch 5)* אַחַת, אֲחָדוֹת

eat, consume *(A.I.E. Ch 2)* א־כ־ל (פָּעַל)

– cause to eat, feed *(B.I.F.B. Ch 10)* (הִפְעִיל)

there is/are not, there is/are none *(A.I.E. Ch 7)* אֵין

man *m (B.I.F.B. Ch 3)* אִישׁ, אֲנָשִׁים

to, toward *(B.I.F.B. Ch 3)* אֶל

God *m (A.I.E. Ch 5)* אֵל

God *m (A.I.E. Ch 4)* אֱלֹהִים

mother *f (A.I.E. Ch 5)* אֵם, אִמּוֹת & אִמָּהוֹת

firmness, support, faithfulness, trust *(A.I.E. Ch 10)* א־מ־ן

– trust, believe *(B.I.F.B. Ch 10)* (הִפְעִיל)

say, utter, tell *(B.I.F.B. Ch 1)* א־מ־ר (פָּעַל)

truth *f (A.I.E. Ch 4)* אֱמֶת, אֲמִתּוֹת

we *(A.I.E. Ch 2)* אֲנַחְנוּ, אָנוּ

men, people (plural of אִישׁ) *m (B.I.F.B. Ch 3)* אֲנָשִׁים

earth, land *f (A.I.E. Ch 3)* אֶרֶץ, אֲרָצוֹת

woman, wife *f (B.I.F.B. Ch 3)* אִשָּׁה, נָשִׁים

who, that, which *(A.I.E. Ch 8)* אֲשֶׁר

woman of, wife of (word pair form of אִשָּׁה) *f (B.I.F.B. Ch 3)* אֵשֶׁת

definite direct object marker (untranslatable) *(A.I.E. Ch 4)* אֶת

with (preposition) *(B.I.F.B. Ch 3)* אֶת

you *m sg (A.I.E. Ch 1)* אַתָּה

ב

with, in (attached preposition) *(A.I.E. Ch 6)* בְּ־, בַּ־

choose, select *(A.I.E. Ch 4)* ב־ח־ר (פָּעַל)

between, among *(B.I.F.B. Ch 1)* בֵּין

house *m (A.I.E. Ch 6)* בַּיִת, בָּתִּים

son, child *m (A.I.E. Ch 3)* בֵּן, בָּנִים

build *(B.I.F.B. Ch 5)* ב־נ־ה

morning *m (B.I.F.B. Ch 1)* בֹּקֶר, בְּקָרִים

create *(A.I.E. Ch 3)* ב־ר־א (פָּעַל)

Creation, in the beginning *(A.I.E. Ch 8)* בְּרֵאשִׁית

bless *(A.I.E. Ch 1)* ב־ר־ך (פָּעַל)

blessed *(A.I.E. Ch 1)* בָּרוּךְ, בְּרוּכָה, בְּרוּכִים, בְּרוּכוֹת

covenant *f (A.I.E. Ch 3)* בְּרִית, בְּרִיתוֹת

ג

mighty, valiant, courageous *adj (A.I.E. Ch 10)* גִּבּוֹר, גִּבּוֹרָה, גִּבּוֹרִים, גִּבּוֹרוֹת

strength, valor, might *f (A.I.E. Ch 10)* גְּבוּרָה, גְּבוּרוֹת

big, great *adj (A.I.E. Ch 5)* גָּדוֹל, גְּדוֹלָה, גְּדוֹלִים, גְּדוֹלוֹת

nation, people *m (A.I.E. Ch 8)* גּוֹי, גּוֹיִים

ד

speak, talk *(A.I.E. Ch 6)* ד־ב־ר (פָּעַל)

word, speech *m (A.I.E. Ch 10)* דָּבָר, דְּבָרִים

thing *m (B.I.F.B. Ch 9)*

blood *m (B.I.F.B. Ch 3)* דָּם, דָּמִים